OTHER TITLES OF INTEREST FROM ST. LUCIE PRESS

Quality Government: Designing, Developing, and Implementing TQM

Teams in Government

Transformational Leadership in Government

Improving Service Quality: Achieving High Performance in the Public and Private Sectors

Total Productivity Management: A Step Beyond TQM and Reengineering

How to Reengineer Your Performance Management Process

Organizational Transformation and Process Reengineering

Sustaining High Performance: The Strategic Transformation to a Customer-Focused Learning Organization

Total Quality Service: Principles, Practices, and Implementation

The Executive Guide to Implementing Quality Systems

Focused Quality: Managing for Results

Principles of Total Quality

Total Quality Management: Text, Cases, and Readings, 2nd Edition

Quality Improvement Handbook: Team Guide to Tools and Techniques

Introduction to Modern Statistical Quality Control and Management

Total Quality in Information Systems and Technology

Total Quality and Organization Development

Total Quality in Managing Human Resources

Total Quality in Purchasing and Supplier Management

Total Quality in Research and Development

For more information about these titles call, fax or write:

St. Lucie Press
100 E. Linton Blvd., Suite 403B
Delray Beach, FL 33483
TEL (407) 274-9906 • FAX (407) 274-9927

S^{t}L

for Treasury's continuous improvement
New Perspectives Group 12-96

CONTINUAL IMPROVEMENT IN GOVERNMENT

TOOLS & METHODS

CONTINUAL IMPROVEMENT IN GOVERNMENT
TOOLS & METHODS

JERRY W. KOEHLER
JOSEPH M. PANKOWSKI

S^t L
St. Lucie Press
Delray Beach, Florida

Printed and bound in the U.S.A. Printed on acid-free paper.
10 9 8 7 6 5 4 3 2 1

ISBN 1-57444-017-9

Direct all inquiries to St. Lucie Press, Inc., 100 E. Linton Blvd., Suite 403B, Delray Beach, Florida 33483.

Phone: (407) 274-9906
Fax: (407) 274-9927

StL

Published by
St. Lucie Press
100 E. Linton Blvd., Suite 403B
Delray Beach, FL 33483

TABLE OF CONTENTS

ABOUT THE AUTHORS

Dr. Jerry W. Koehler recently returned to the faculty in the Department of Management at the University of South Florida in Tampa after serving the past three years as Deputy Secretary in the Florida Department of Labor and Employment Security.

Dr. Koehler has authored numerous books and has served as consultant to government agencies and leading business organizations. He is co-author with Joseph Pankowski of another book, *Quality Government: Designing, Developing and Implementing TQM*, (St. Lucie Press, 1996), and two additional St. Lucie titles, *Teams in Government* and *Leadership in Government.*

Joseph M. Pankowski is no stranger to quality improvement efforts, having directed the Bureau of Quality Assurance in the Florida Department of Labor and Security for five years prior to working with Dr. Koehler. He continues serving as a consultant to the Department on quality management, and conducts seminars on customer expectations, teams, tools, and presentation skills.

During his 31 years of work with government, he has experience as a first-line rehabilitation counselor, state supervisor and assistant director, in addition to other assignments. He has directed teams studying innovative approaches in service delivery, and under his guidance the Bureau of Quality Assurance was recognized by the federal government for its excellence.

1 INTRODUCTION

Government organizations are experiencing dramatic change. Many are moving from traditional methods of managing to a quality perspective, where the focus is on the customer, continual improvement of processes, the team approach, and processes driven by accurate and meaningful data. In the early 1990s, we accepted the challenge of implementing Total Quality Management in the Department of Revenue and the Department of Labor and Employment Security in the State of Florida. A complete description of how we implemented TQM in government can be found in our book *Total Quality Government: Designing, Developing and Implementing Total Quality Management* by St. Lucie Press.

Our purpose in writing this book is to describe in detail how quality organizations in government collect and use data to continually improve government processes. Our aim is to provide a book that clearly identifies quality tools and methods, and the steps necessary to employ them in government organizations. We have tested every tool and method in this book in a government setting and have found their application to be extremely beneficial in improving processes.

How organizational members use these tools will differ significantly. Each tool and method is extremely valuable. However, our approach to continual improvement in government was largely based upon teams. Therefore, we take the position that quality tools and methods are interrelated and therefore, all team members should be competent in using all quality tools and methods. The choice of tools and methods is governed in large measure by teams composed of organizational members, which we refer to as "associates." Their mission is to continually improve the processes to which they are assigned.

When we began implementing process improvement teams in government, we realized that many team members had limited analytical skills, little understanding of mathematics and even less knowledge of statistics. It was not uncommon to have the majority of members on a team whose education was complete at the high school level. Dedicated as they were to finding solutions to their problems, they truly feared any mention of numbers, data collection or mathematical charts. Even those with Bachelor's or Master's degrees were often not comfortable working with statistics. Our intent in this book is to reduce these fears and provide a clear, simple approach to collecting and analyzing data for improving government processes.

Many government organizations are now finding that people working together in teams, as opposed to just working on a single task, have been very successful in improving the way work gets done. We have observed dramatic results when process improvement teams are instituted in government organizations. Teams are most successful when they focus on the customers of their processes, flow chart their processes and allow data collected with the assistance of quality tools to drive their decisions. Not all teams are successful, and from our experience the number one reason for lack of team success is the team's inability to use tools and methods in collecting and analyzing data and in making decisions.

Continual process improvement requires data collection and analysis, and successful teams understand when and how to use quality tools when the occasion demands their use. Just as an electrician or plumber may use some tools on a daily basis and others rarely, teams should also use appropriate tools that help them to improve a process. We found that when introducing tools and methods to a new continual improvement team, the following principles should be stressed:

A. Work in government organizations can best be understood and improved if activities are composed of processes.

B. Government processes involve activities that can be improved.

C. The goal of each process is to meet or exceed customer expectations.

D. Continual improvement produces lasting results.

E. Continual improvement requires understanding of a process.

F. People closest to the process are in the best position to improve it.

G. Measurement of each process is essential.

H. Graphic problem solving works best with processes that are charted.

I. Decisions to improve the process are data-based.

J. Understanding and applying continual improvement tools and methods facilitate problem solving.

There are shelves of textbooks devoted to the subject of data collection, and the reader is encouraged to refer to them as necessary. The intent of this introduction to tools and methods is not to prepare one to present dissertation findings before a university doctoral committee, but rather to provide an overview and introduction to tools that will facilitate process improvements in the workplace. What may seem elementary to a few experienced readers will be very beneficial to others who may not have prior experience with formal instruction in tools and methods of TQM. With this introduction, the student who wishes more detail on a particular tool or method can go to the library knowing what to look for and where to find it.

At the heart of Total Quality Management is data. Data drives decisions. Organization members should not make decisions based upon hunches, collective wisdom or what the boss likes. Unfortunately, in many organizations and particularly in government, managers do not make decisions based upon data. They often lack faith in the data they have or do not have quality data given to them.

WHAT IS QUALITY DATA?

Quality data is verifiable, accurate and meaningful. It is also timely, valid and reliable.

HOW DO WE COLLECT QUALITY DATA?

Quality data is collected through surveys, process indicators, documented observations, research and the use of TQM tools.

HOW DO WE USE QUALITY DATA?

Although data collection and analysis can have multiple applications, including reports to funding sources (budgets, etc.), quality data is used in TQM to *improve processes.*

To improve processes requires effective decision-making...
Effective decision-making begins with accurate data...

Therefore we use quality data to

- identify problems in the process,
- measure process improvements,
- establish base-line data,
- provide feedback to associates working on the process,
- prevent problems,
- set priorities, and
- compare processes.

HOW DO WE DISPLAY DATA?

The purpose of displaying data is to share results with all associates working on the process. Therefore, data is not guarded and kept secret by top management, but is available to everyone. Individuals working on the process should have easy access to the data and have associates available to answer any questions they might have. The data should be displayed on graphs and in flowcharts posted on bulletin boards with telephone numbers for answers to questions.

The collection, analysis, display and use of quality data is the backbone of Total Quality Management. The days of computer printouts filled with statistics stored in files or stacked on shelves in the computer system libraries are over. As teams begin using quality data, they will demand that the data not only be readily available, but be meaningful in terms of the processes under study.

ONE FINAL WORD ABOUT DATA

On occasion, team members wonder what data should be collected and analyzed. They might ask why they should even gather more data if sufficient data is already available from their data center. The answer is relatively simple:

1. What is important to the customers? Look at your flowcharts. Where are the problems? Where are your customers complaining?
2. Is there already data collected at these points?

3. If "yes," is the data trustworthy? Is the data timely?
4. If "yes," use it. If not, collect new data based upon what is important to the customers.

WHAT IF OUR TEAM FAILS TO ACHIEVE PROCESS IMPROVEMENT?

Most process improvement initiatives do some good. If by chance the wrong tool, method or data is used, the process will still probably improve. Total Quality Management has been used in hospitals throughout the world, and there is not one documented case where a patient died because of a team's process improvement. If the analysis does not involve "life and death" decisions, whatever improvements occur will far outweigh any potential risk damage to the process. Remember that Total Quality Management is a series of unending, small improvements made by teams of people working to enhance customer satisfaction. The tools and methods on the following pages are designed to achieve this goal. Use them as needed. No team will probably use all, or even half, of the ones covered. However, many will remain "in the bottom of your tool box" waiting for the right application.

WHAT IF OUR TEAM NEEDS HELP?

Call for help. Later, we will discuss "process improvement guides" that were used by our agency. You may wish to consider calling in a statistician, if necessary, to help with the more complicated tools. Contact your local community college. There are lots of people interested in quality improvements and who can offer help.

There are actually twenty traditional tools and methods for continual improvement contained in this workbook. Two additional entries, "Time Management" and "World Wide Web" have been added because of their value to teams. In addition we have included "Blue Chips," our way of saying that these extras are a bonus worth reading when you have time.

Often, the hardest part of beginning anything new is just that—beginning. Once you and your team are underway, the going will get a bit easier. So, to quote a well-known shoemaker—just do it!

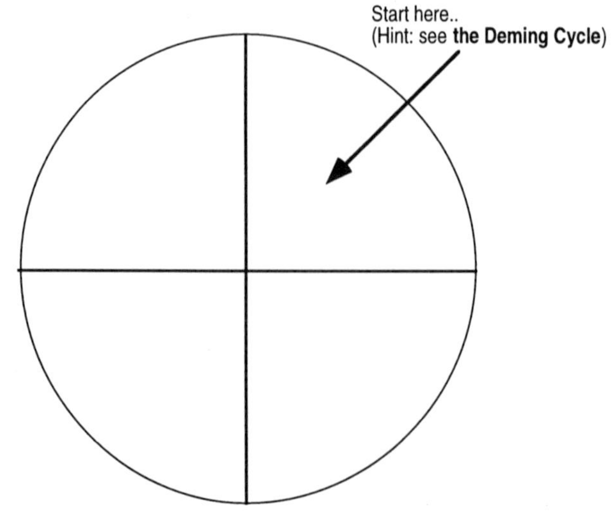

Guide to Appropriate Tools

What tools are appropriate for answering the following questions?

• •

What problem should we look at first?
(2, 3, 6, 8, 14, 15, 16, 17)

How do we collect and chart the frequency of occurrence, relative importance, kind of error, or potential sources of poor quality?
(4, 5, 6, 10, 15, 16, 18, 19)

How do we compare our service delivery or products to others? (1)

How can a team come up with possible reasons for a problem or possible solutions?
(2, 3, 6, 14, 15, 16, 20)

How do we examine the possible relationship(s) between various causes of a problem? (2, 3)

How can we show the positive and negative forces affecting a problem? (9)

What do we need to know to make a presentation to the Quality Council? (12)

1. Benchmarking
2. Brainstorming
3. Cause and Effect Diagrams
4. Check Sheets
5. Control Chart
6. Customer Surveys
7. Deming Cycle
8. Flowcharts
9. Force Field Analysis
10. Histograms
11. Introducing Change
12. Management Presentations
13. Milestone Charts
14. Nominal Group Method
15. Pareto Charts
16. Pie Charts
17. Priority Selection Worksheets
18. Run Charts
19. Scatter Diagram
20. Solution Strategies Matrix
21. Time Management
22. World Wide Web

2 BENCHMARKING

We have presented the tools and methods of Total Quality Management in alphabetical order so they will be easy to locate. Thus "benchmarking" will come early (first), and towards the back will be tools like "solution strategies matrix" and "time management." On the other hand, it has been our experience that benchmarking is not the most often used of the tools and methods. This is disappointing since there is real merit in this tool.

When someone mentions "benchmarking," what is the first image that comes to mind? A bench? Perhaps a mark on a bench? Maybe carpenters place marks on their work benches to serve as quality guides as they cut boards for tables? We're getting close to the definition.

WHAT IS IT?

Benchmarking is a way of comparing your processes to those of a recognized leader, in order to identify gaps.

WHY SHOULD IT BE USED?

If you know how you measure up against competitors, it may be possible to study your processes to see how they can be improved to exceed the competition.

A good example of benchmarking can be found with the Xerox Corporation. For years, Xerox led the world in the manufacture of superb copiers. Yet, when competition heated up from copier manufacturers in Japan, it was evident that to stay competitive Xerox had to intensify its efforts to be the best. They implemented benchmarking.

Benchmarking consists of a series of several steps. Quality experts differ on the number of steps and exact descriptions of benchmarking (as they do for all the tools), but the following components are found in most:

Step One

Identify the subject and key characteristics of the benchmarking. For example, an agency interested in accurate eligibility decisions for disability insurance based upon criteria set by the federal government might use an error rate supplied by the Social Security Administration.

Step Two

Identify who you will benchmark—other agencies, companies or organizations—and collect data. In our example above, we would likely select agencies in other states performing the same work. We would look for "the best," or those whose error rates are lower than ours.

Step Three

Analyze the reasons for the gaps that exist between your program and the best. Examine your processes (using teams who do the work) to see where improvements can be made. Examine what the best does that makes them the best. Constantly improve and examine your processes.

The Xerox Corporation won the Malcolm Baldrige National Quality Award in 1989. In its publication *Leadership Through Quality Processes and Tools Review*, Xerox presented its concept of benchmarking ("Quality You Can Copy") as in the model below:

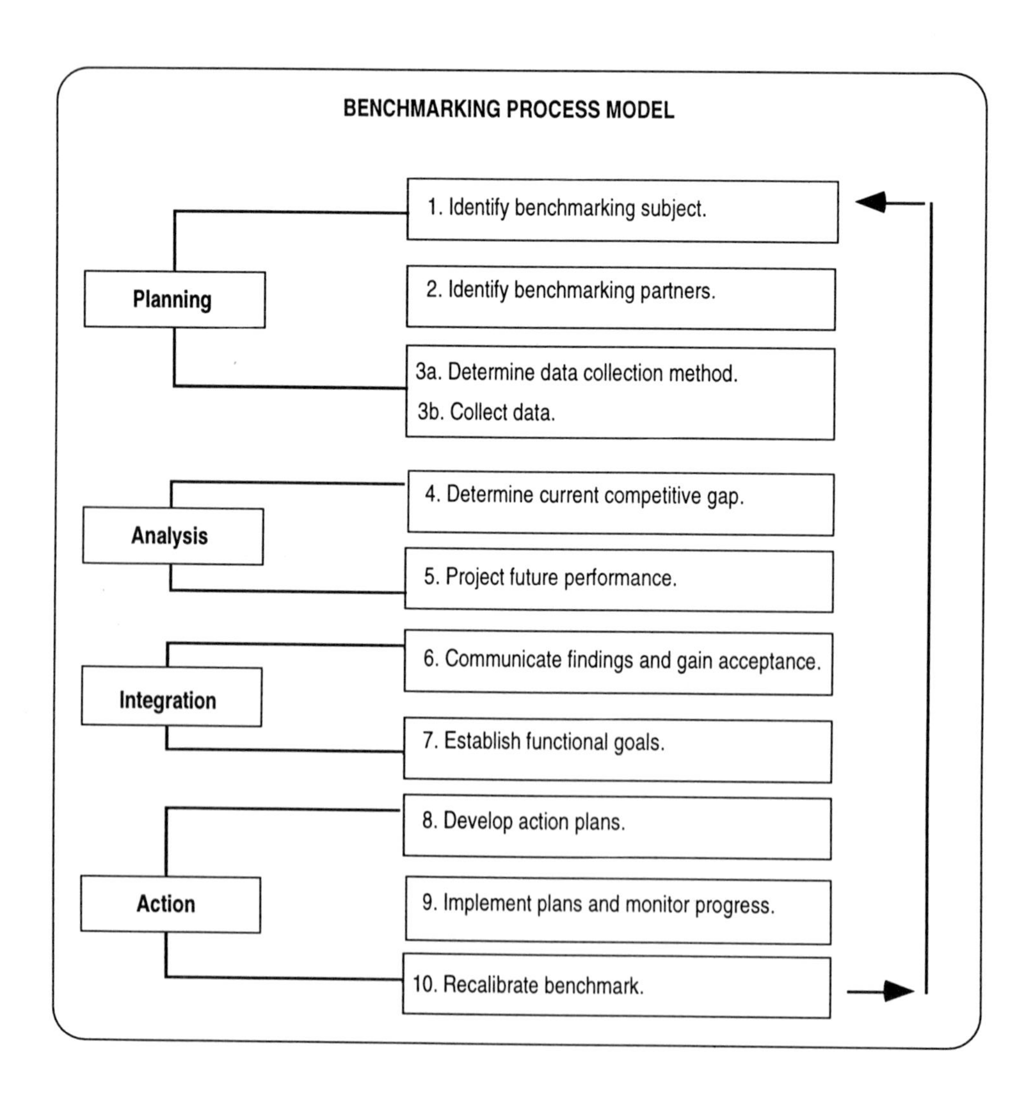

DISCUSSION

It has been our experience that benchmarking is not often done by teams who work in government. Excuses for not using benchmarking frequently include:

"There is no other program like ours..."

"Other states have more money to work with.."

"They have a different personnel plan with more flexibility..."

"Our staff does not have the training resources the other agencies have..."

Many of these excuses stem from a fear of benchmarking, including the concern that weaknesses in their own program will be highlighted by comparing it with an outstanding one. In a true TQM organization, this is exactly the objective. In a true TQM organization, management will have "driven out fear" in keeping with Dr. Deming's principles, and every effort will be made to improve the process.

Another concern centers on a fear of not knowing what should be selected to benchmark. Should an agency look at the number of successful job placements? Time taken to serve their customer? The number of referrals received from their community? Cost of services? Overhead administrative costs? The number of customers served as a percentage of those referred?

The answer is that any one or more of these measures can be benchmark. A good idea of what should be can be found in the mission statement and vision for the agency. What does the agency claim to do? What is important to the customers served? Which customers? For example, one customer, the one walking in the door for services, would certainly be interested in their chances for successful placement if they are in an employment jobs office. Yet another, the firm placing job orders with the agency, would be interested in having "quality" referrals, whose experience and skills will ensure a long-term successful placement.

Care, therefore, must be taken in selecting the measures that will be benchmarked. A good place to begin is in the reports that are already prepared for your program to meet requirements imposed by funding sources. For example, the federal government has established a number of measures that are required by states in obtaining matching dollars. Other measures have been developed to meet state requirements, and are readily available from your headquarters' data management system.

See how these reports compare to the mission and vision developed in your agency. Your office in the field might be able to benchmark against others judged "best the state," i.e., the one with the lowest error rate.

Example

The following example demonstrates how benchmarking was used in actual practice.

The Division of Unemployment Compensation in the Florida Department of Labor and Employment Security discussed some of its benchmarks in their application for the Sterling Award:

> We compare our state with other states, nationally and regionally in addition to size and population. Historical data is also used to determine excellence in specific offices throughout the state. By identifying these "best in class" situations, we can review differences in processes, identify successful factors, and set goals for process improvement in other areas. One major process improvement was the implementation of a voice response telephone system to provide our customers with easy access to information concerning the status of their benefit payments. The voice response team contacted several other states who were successfully using this technology. Industry was studied, and a benchmark was established based on the most successful systems.

Display

Benchmarks are often displayed graphically in the following manner:

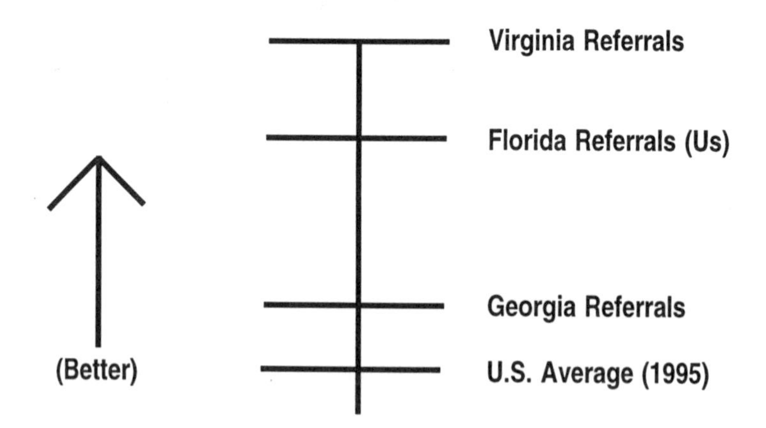

SUMMARY

- Benchmarking is a tool that enables you to compare your internal organizational processes and end results with the best in your industry or organizations.
- Look for the best, leaders in the field.
- Compare your performance with the best.
- Make improvements.
- Compare again.

3 BRAINSTORMING

While the first tool, benchmarking, is used infrequently, **brainstorming** is probably used the most often because it is so much fun.

We have always stressed that quality improvement should be fun, and that if a team is not enjoying the experience, they are probably doing something wrong. That is not to say that work is not also involved in process improvement. It's just that when a team is "on target," "in the flow," or "firing on all cylinders," it *is* fun. People are generally social animals and enjoy working together in groups. They especially enjoy brainstorming.

WHAT IS IT?

Brainstorming is a way of generating a number of possible solutions to a problem. It stresses the use of "open-minded" or "free thinking" without critique of any idea expressed. The goal of brainstorming is to come up with as many ideas as possible without regard to "quality," with as many team members as possible contributing their thoughts.

Remember, the central concept of brainstorming is the great number of possible solutions with the agreement by all members that no criticisms are allowed of any idea expressed. The quantity of ideas is far more important than the quality of ideas.

WHY SHOULD IT BE USED?

The best way to solve problems is to consider all possible solutions. The word "all" is used loosely here, because it is unlikely that any team will ever list every conceivable solution to a problem. Nevertheless, brainstorming does ensure that people do begin their problem solving with an open mind and not focus in on the "obvious" or "usual" answers to a problem. Often the obvious or usual answers are not the best.

WHAT DOES A TEAM NEED TO USE IT?

There are just a few things that should be made available to the team. These include:

- At least two people, not necessarily team members, who will volunteer to serve as recorders (Ideas will often be generated very rapidly, and one recorder may be overcome).
- Several flip charts with decent markers (The markers should be relatively new and dark-colored).
- Masking tape (The tape may be used to hold the flip chart pages to a wall).

Some teams like to work under time guidelines, and a clock might be needed to time the session. A facilitator would also be helpful in brainstorming, especially if the team elects to use the "structured" method. We found that team leaders make teams follow the rules in most cases. The rules follow the discussion of "structured" vs. "unstructured" brainstorming.

WHAT ELSE DO WE NEED TO KNOW?

Technically there are two kinds of brainstorming—structured and unstructured.

Structured: The leader or facilitator controls and directs the group more in the structured brainstorming session and asks each member, in turn, to suggest an idea or "pass" until the next round. Every member is therefore required to participate by either giving an idea or passing. This method forces even the least vocal member to participate and ensures that no one member can dominate the discussion. On the other hand, some team members might not appreciate the pressure to respond regularly.

Unstructured: In this type of brainstorming, members suggest ideas as they come to mind. There is no "circle" of required discussion, and no one is required to respond "pass" if they have no idea. Unfortunately, the disadvantage of this approach is that there may be two or three more vocal people who dominate the discussion. Perhaps the more reserved member might have the very best ideas.

HOW DO WE DO IT? WHAT ARE THE RULES?

First, know that there are many approaches to brainstorming. Most include the following steps:

Step One

The leader or facilitator explains the topic, process or problem that will be brainstormed. The recorder writes it on the flip chart.

Step Two

The leader or facilitator gives a brief overview of brainstorming and the key rules:

- offer as many ideas as you can—be creative
- build on other ideas if you wish
- offer absolutely no criticism at any time, (even positive feedback is not allowed)
- every idea will be placed on the flip chart in the exact words of the contributor
- no discussion of any idea is allowed until all members have exhausted ideas

Step Three

Begin. When all ideas have been presented, a number of other methods can be used to clarify the ideas, to consider the relative merit of each (rank order), and to determine how each might be combined with others and what to do with them.

EXAMPLE

There is a story told of a small town in Maine that was experiencing tremendous problems with snow and ice. It seems that ice would form on the electrical power lines during winter storms causing them to break under the load. The town leaders decided to "brainstorm" a solution...

"Let's shake the snow off the lines, but how do we do it?"

"Just shake the poles, that's how..."

"The poles are frozen in the ground, but we could get bears to climb them."

"How do we do that?"

"Put honey pots on the top of every pole. Just get them to go for the sweet honey in the honey pots at the top!"

"But how do we get the pots on the top of the poles?"

"We could lower the honey pots to the top of the poles if we had a helicopter."

"But where do we get one of them things?"

"The National Guard has one! They can lower the honey pots!"

The problem was solved. The town leaders got the National Guard to fly over the poles and the power lines without having to wake up the hibernating bears. The "down draft" from the whirling blades blew the snow off the power lines.

4 CAUSE AND EFFECT DIAGRAMS

Several years ago, one of the authors of this workbook built a wooden deck at his home in the woods of northern Florida. The deck was well-constructed; however, after a few years, the railings surrounding the deck began to warp. Not only did the rails pitch from side to side, but they also twisted and turned. Several causes were suggested for this problem. Perhaps the builder used poor quality wood. Perhaps he failed to refer to proper plans or used the wrong tools. In an effort to identify the cause or causes for this problem, the author turned to a very useful tool—the "cause and effect" diagram.

WHAT IS IT?

The **Cause and Effect diagram**, also known as the "fish-bone" diagram, can be used to identify all potential causes of a given problem. The diagram represents the relationship between an effect (problem) and its potential causes. It is used to identify, explore and display all of the possible causes of a specific problem or condition. The team first "brainstorms" all possible causes, often spends time between meetings to uncover other reasons for the problem, and then constructs the diagram. Additional brainstorming sessions may be used to minimize the chance of overlooking one or more causes.

WHY SHOULD IT BE USED?

Most problems have multiple causes, some of which interact with each other. Although brainstorming helps identify these causes, the cause and effect diagram displays the causes and shows the interaction that may be occurring.

WHAT DOES A TEAM NEED TO USE IT?

The major requirements are those that make brainstorming effective. Refer to the discussion on brainstorming for these "rules." The only other requirements are a volunteer to serve as recorder, a flip chart and several dark-colored markers.

HOW DO WE DO IT? WHAT ARE THE RULES?

Know that when we refer to the "rules," we only mean "principles" or "guidelines." Team members often construct outstanding charts and diagrams without conforming to rules or mandates from authors of books. That being said, the following is offered as guidance:

Step One

Draw a box. Within this box, write the name of the problem you are addressing. For example,

The rails look awful!

Step Two

This is where it gets a little more complicated. Here team members are asked to identify the "categories" into which the causes will be placed. Often, cause and effect diagrams have four major categories—people, materials, machines, and process (or method). These cover a wealth of potential major categories, but cause and effect diagrams may have many more than four major categories, including "environment," "measurements," and "hardware." Do not worry about this now. Just try for four major categories.

Step Three

Follow the steps and rules for brainstorming to come up with as many potential causes as possible for your problem. The recorder should attempt to place each into one of the major categories. Do not worry if it is difficult to fit the cause into one of the categories vs. another. That can come later.

Step Four

Draw your diagram. Discuss the causes again. See if any fit into more than one category (interconnections). See if any can be eliminated. Discuss which are the most likely causes. Recommend which ones the team should pursue to correct, and which are beyond the team's control (and referred to someone else, perhaps management).

EXAMPLE

Because we began discussion of the cause and effect diagram with the "awful rails," we will pursue this example. (This particular diagram has been used extensively in our training program, and classes are always able to identify the exact cause of the railings problem. Can you?)

What caused the "awful rails?"

Cause	Category
• "The builder did not know what he was doing."	People
• "The boards were the wrong ones."	Materials
• "Wrong nails."	Materials
• "The builder was rushed."	People
• "No plans were used."	Process
• "Bad saw."	Machines
• "Boards were not waterproofed."	Process
• "No level was used."	Process
• "The builder was too proud to ask directions."	People
• "The earth is settling."	Materials (?)
• "Lousy hammer."	Machines
• "No paint was used."	Process

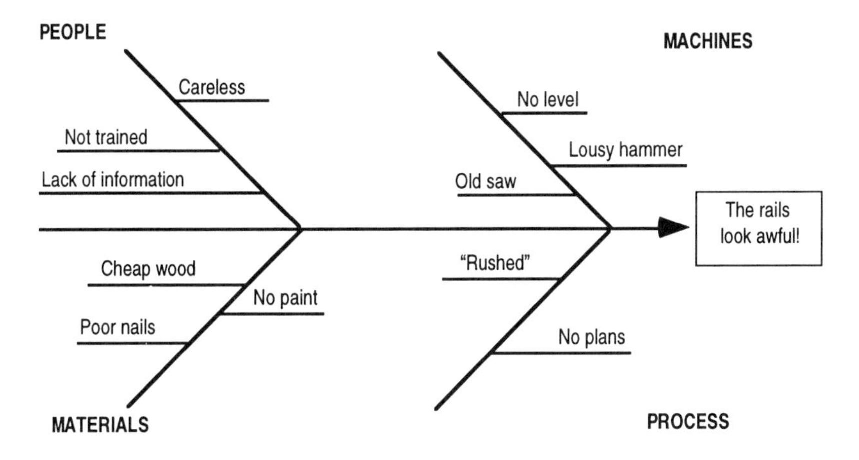

The cause? The major cause was a lack of paint (or sealant) to keep the water from soaking the wood (which caused it to warp).

Another example of a cause and effect diagram may be seen in one developed by a team examining "excessive waiting time" in a Department of Labor and Employment Security Office:

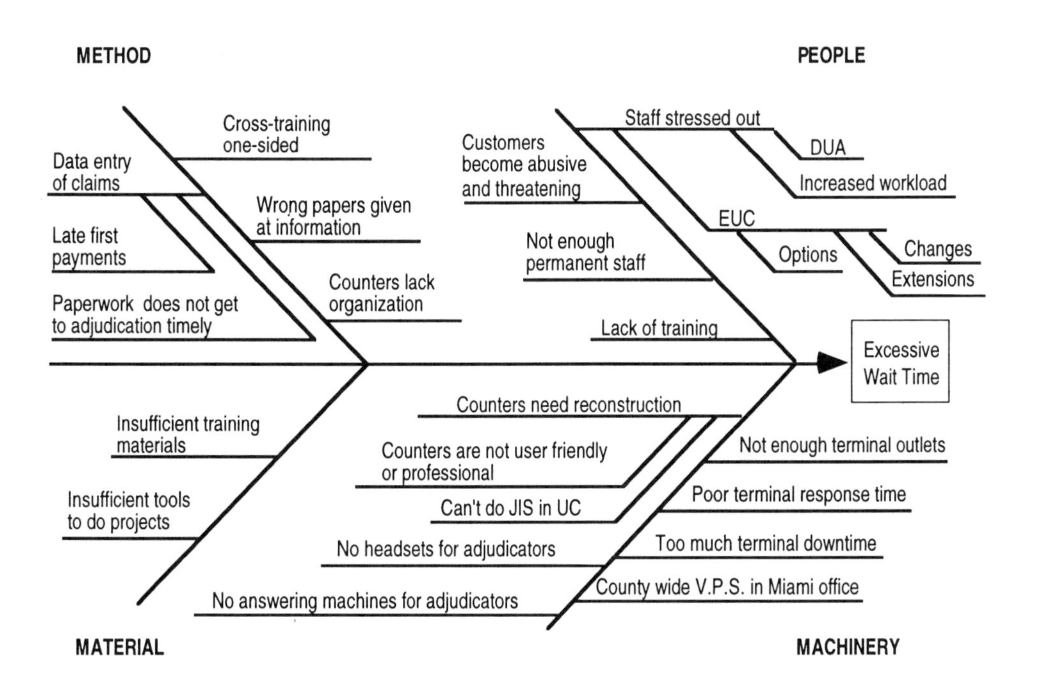

BLUE CHIPS

- Remember that the cause and effect diagram will help the team identify possible, or likely, causes of problems based on "gut level" responses. It will be necessary to verify these feelings with hard data collected with customer surveys, obtained from a mainframe computer or discovered in other ways. Making improvements based only on perceptions can be very risky.
- Use the cause and effect diagram only after a process has been flowcharted, and the problem is well-defined. It is a good idea to place a completed diagram on a wall next to the break room or in another place where others can see it and react. Later, when we discuss flowcharting, we will also suggest doing this with that chart. The more people who see what the team is working on, the better. They may come up with many good suggestions.
- The cause and effect diagram can also be used by a team to identify things that must occur if a successful solution is to be achieved. In this way the cause and effect diagram becomes a "positive" chart, no longer showing cause for a problem, but elements needed to insure success.

An example of this is:

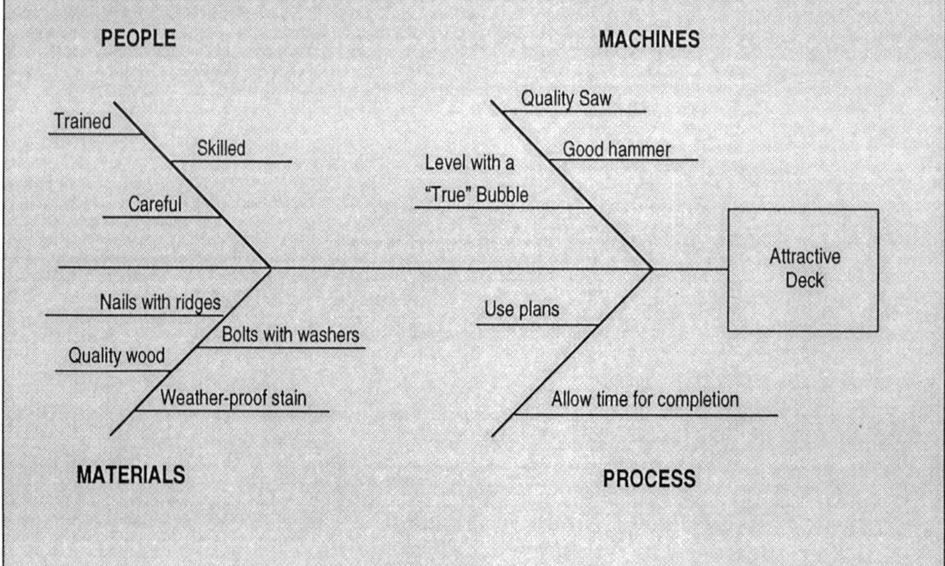

5 CHECK SHEETS

Many team members may have little experience collecting data. Some fear anything to do with numbers as a result of a bad experience with "arithmetic," algebra or statistics when they were in school. A major goal of this workbook is to take the mystery out of anything associated with continual improvement or Total Quality Management. Much of that mystery or fear is associated with the collection or analysis of data. We will try to simplify this process.

WHAT IS IT?

A **check sheet** is a tool designed to make certain that the data is collected and analyzed in a standard way. The check sheet organizes the collection of data. With this order it is easier for all members of the team to understand what has been collected and what conclusions might be drawn from an analysis of the data.

WHY SHOULD IT BE USED?

The major uses for the check sheet, in addition to organizing collected data, are to help the team begin to find patterns in the data and to begin finding areas where problems may be concentrated.

WHAT DOES A TEAM NEED TO USE IT?

The major task in using a check sheet, other than collecting the data, is determining the data to be displayed and the design of the sheet. Therefore, before designing the check sheet and collecting the data, the team will have to decide what they consider important and what they wish to measure. The team may refer to the flowchart they have developed from the process under consideration, or may examine their cause and effect diagram to see where data may be collected.

HOW DO WE DO IT? WHAT ARE THE RULES?

Before beginning, let us add the following caution. Just as is true with many of the other methods and tools discussed in this workbook, there is no one absolute way to construct a check sheet. For example, a book by Juran, or one by a statistician you might locate at your local university, will undoubtedly show differences in what is referred to as a check sheet. Disregard these minor details. Just follow the sequence below, and you will be on target.

Step One

Define the reason why the data is being collected. Obtain agreement from the team as to what will be collected and recorded.

Step Two

Decide how long and when the data will be collected. The team may wish to collect the data hourly, daily, weekly, monthly or over another period of time. Data might be collected only in the mornings or afternoons. Much depends on what you are looking at and how costly it will be to collect the data.

Step Three

Design a data collection form. There are many ways to design the form depending upon need. A few examples of forms follow the last step. Make the form as easy to use as is possible. Do not make it too complex with information that can be obtained elsewhere (i.e., you do not need to list the job title of the data collector). Do include space to list the name of the recorder, dates, place and observations recorded, and other information that is essential. Leave enough "white space" for the recorder to write any special information about the data.

Step Four

Field-testing the check sheet to see if it works is one of the most critical steps, but is often skipped "in the interest of time." Too often the check sheet is developed by a team and distributed to the recorders the same afternoon. Only after it is used does the team discover an error in the check sheet or some very important omission. It is wise to take time to test the check sheet to see if anything needs to be changed or improved before the actual survey begins.

Step Five

Examine the check sheet to make sure instructions and categories are clearly written for the recorder. Are all terms easy to understand? Do any require a definition so that the data will be standardized across several recorders? Does the recorder know what to do when something special comes up? Who makes the final judgment calls? Does the recorder know who the judge is? How does one contact the judge?

Step Six

Recorders collect and record the data.

Step Seven

Analyze the data.

EXAMPLES

DELAYS IN ELIGIBILITY DETERMINATION

Date__________ Notes: ____________________

Recorder

"Why does it take so long to make an eligibility determination?"

Reasons Given by Counselors	Tally	Total
Transportation problems (making arrangements, etc.)	~~IIII~~ II	7
Missed appointments	~~IIII~~ ~~IIII~~ ~~IIII~~ ~~IIII~~ I	21
Waiting for medical/psychological appointments	~~IIII~~ ~~IIII~~ ~~IIII~~ ~~IIII~~ ~~IIII~~ ~~IIII~~ ~~IIII~~ ~~IIII~~ IIII	44
Waiting for medical/psychological/vocational evaluation reports	~~IIII~~ ~~IIII~~ ~~IIII~~ ~~IIII~~ ~~IIII~~ ~~IIII~~ ~~IIII~~	35
Waiting for consultation with consultants	~~IIII~~ ~~IIII~~	10
Overload of work (backlog created by large caseloads)	~~IIII~~	5
Complexity of problems require more time	II	2

Customer Service—Division of Unemployment Compensation
Bureau of Claims and Benefits

Date __________ Recorder __________

Notes ____________________

1. I feel that when I reported to the Unemployment Claims Office:

	Very Good	Good	Adequate	Poor	Unsatisfactory
A. Courtesy shown to me was...	IIII	~~IIII~~ ~~IIII~~ ~~IIII~~	~~IIII~~	II	
B. Waiting time for service was...	~~IIII~~ III	~~IIII~~ ~~IIII~~ ~~IIII~~	III		
C. Instructions for filing my claim were...	~~IIII~~ I	~~IIII~~ ~~IIII~~ ~~IIII~~	IIII		

2. How much time did you spend in the claims office on your first visit?

Under 1 Hour	1-2 Hours	2-3 Hours	Over 3 Hours
~~IIII~~ ~~IIII~~ IIII	~~IIII~~ ~~IIII~~	I	

3. What is the travel time one way from your home to the claims office?

Under 1 Hour	1-2 Hours	Over 2 Hours
~~IIII~~ ~~IIII~~ ~~IIII~~	~~IIII~~ IIII	

Another interesting way to develop a check sheet would be to take a copy of your flowchart or cause and effect diagram, and place the check marks directly on the chart. Or you may wish to develop a check sheet showing errors on an application form by tabulating the errors right on the form:

Name: 𝍸 II

Address: 𝍸 𝍸 I

City: II State: ZIP: 𝍸 III

Social Security # 𝍸 𝍸 𝍸 II

Driver's License # III

Date of Birth: 𝍸 𝍸 Height: III Weight: 𝍸

Job Classification: 𝍸 𝍸 𝍸 II

Home Telephone #: 𝍸 𝍸 𝍸 𝍸 III

One final example of an interesting check sheet is one that makes use of a drawing. Perhaps the team is interested in tracking damages on incoming boxes of reports from field offices. By placing check marks on the parts of a diagram of the incoming boxes, it may be possible to see if any trends exist (like the tops or left sides are always damaged.)

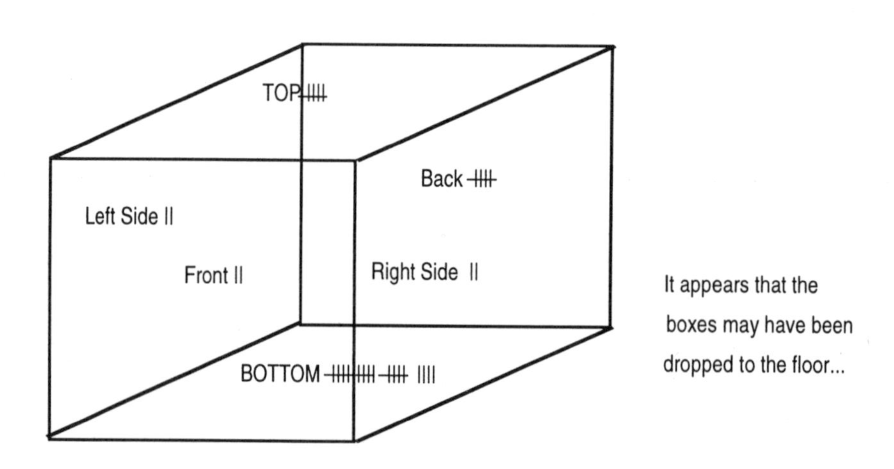

THINGS TO CONSIDER

- Check sheets appear to be one of the easiest tools to use. However, make sure the check sheet is as clear as possible.
- Make sure that all team members, or recorders, are using the same definitions for the data collected.
- All categories should be mutually exclusive so that an entry clearly falls into one or the other. An easy example of an error in this would have categories:

0–**5**

5–10

10–15

Avoid narrative descriptions for categories that confuse both the recorder and customer.

- Watch the type of categories used. A definition for a category might be so broad that all entries will fall into it.
- Keep the check sheet simple and easy to use.
- Use whatever amount of paper is necessary for the data collection. Make it easier by keeping separate check sheets for different recorders, different offices, or different time periods. Keeping these separate may also help the team to spot trends during different months, etc.
- Don't stop collecting data just because the office gets busy or is short on staff. This data may be the most important and crucial to the final analysis.

QUESTIONS

What are we trying to find out about the process with this check sheet?

What kinds of data will help answer these questions?

Who will be asked to provide data? Why?

What will we learn as a result of our analysis?

6 CONTROL CHARTS

Control Charts are intimidating to most team members. Control charts look confusing and open to criticism by others who might know more than you do. So, why would anyone in their right mind want to consider a control chart? Because the control chart is one of the very best ways to demonstrate when a process under study is "out of control." It is a statistically sound way to show this and does not rely on assumptions, perceptions or gut reactions.

If you follow the explanation and examples given in the next few pages, you will be able to construct a control chart that will impress your leaders and provide statistically sound data.

WHAT IS IT?

The **Control Chart** is a Run Chart (you may wish to look up Run Charts before proceeding) that makes use of statistical formulas to define Upper Control Limits (UCL) and Lower Control Limits (LCL). The control chart identifies when a process is out of control, so that the cause(s) can be analyzed. When the process is in control, no effort is made to adjust the process. The UCL and LCL are determined by examining the results of the process by taking samples and using a series of statistical formulas. The goal of the control chart is a simple one—to signal when a process is in or out of control.

WHY SHOULD IT BE USED?

Even the best processes will not produce 100% "ideal" results. There will be some variability present in anything. If the process is in control, however, the variances will fall within the control limits. Outcomes will vary without setting a trend or producing a cycle of any kind. The reasons for these small variabilities are numerous, but of no concern, because they fall within the control limits. One way to influence these minor variances would be to change the system with a new process.

EXAMPLE

Let's consider the number of days it takes for a customer to be enrolled in a work evaluation for a state-supported job training program. Examine the following numbers:

52 55 54 51 46 49
46 47 48 50 60 53
45 57 53 47 57 47
61 55 54 52 51 54
55 53 57 47 57 54

What can we say about this random-looking group of numbers? It appears that most customers spend somewhere between 45 and 61 days waiting to get into a work evaluation. One got lucky and was enrolled in 45 days. Yet another waited 61 days. What do you think of a process that has this range? Is something wrong? Is the process under control? Or is it out of control? What would be an acceptable number of days one customer should be expected to wait? What would be the most number of days anyone should wait? Constructing a control chart will help the team examine and analyze this process.

DISCUSSION

Sometimes when a process is really out of control variances fall way above or below the control limits. If a process is found to be out of control in an agency, it may be due to a change in policy, or perhaps a new supplier was hired who is not familiar with the quality standards. Maybe associates are angry at management, or are just "burned out," caring little about quality. In any event, a process out of control is one in need of attention.

Just because a process is in control does not mean that it is fulfilling customers' needs. It only means that results are consistent. They may be consistently bad. To address the need to meet customers' expectations requires that specifications (upper and lower) be developed, which can be more restrictive than control limits if a genuine quality service is desired. Remember the previous example about the number of days it took for a customer to be enrolled in a work evaluation? There were two numbers (45 days and 61 days) that may be outside control limits. Then we asked what would be an "acceptable" number of waiting days that a customer should not expect to exceed. When we ask this question, we are actually asking what specifications would be appropriate—which is not the same as the upper and lower limits. Specifications are determined according to what we think. Control limits (UCL and LCL) are calculated rather than determined externally. These numbers may be identical, but sometimes our own specifications may be more restrictive.

WHY SHOULD IT BE USED?

Control charts demonstrate vividly that there is variability in every process. About one-half of the data points will tend to be above the mean, and the other half below. Dr. W. Edwards Deming notes that one can always try to minimize the variation by "improving constantly and forever the system of production and service."

WHAT DOES A TEAM NEED TO USE IT?

The first thing that a team should realize is that it is possible to construct a control chart without knowing a lot about statistics. If one follows the examples given in this discussion, it is possible to construct a basic control chart without knowing why the calculations produce it. For those who wish to have a deeper understanding of the process, and the differences between continuous (variables) and discrete (attributes) control charts, it will be necessary for them to refer to other books on statistics. Our discussion will produce a control chart based on the observations mentioned earlier—the number of days it takes for a customer to be enrolled in a work evaluation. We will develop the control chart for (1) the average number of days (X), and (2) for the range (R). A Table of Factors will be used for the formulas.

SUMMARY

1. Collect your data.
2. Follow step by step the following example—using your own data.
3. Take it slow and easy.

HOW DO WE DO IT? WHAT ARE THE RULES?

The following sequence will produce

1. A Control Chart for the Average Observations and
2. A Control Chart for the Range of the Observations

Step One

Place your data in a chart.

	Jan	Feb	Mar	Apr	May	Jun
Number of Days	52	55	54	51	46	49
	46	47	48	50	60	53
	45	57	53	47	57	47
	61	55	54	52	51	54
	55	53	57	47	57	54
Average ($\bar{X}$)	51.8	53.4	53.2	49.4	54.2	51.4
Range (R)	16	10	9	5	14	7
Number of Samples	5	5	5	5	5	5

Step Two

Calculate the average ($\bar{X}$) for each column by adding the column and dividing by the number of observations. For example, in row one (Jan) we add 52, 46, 45, 61, and 55 for a total of 259. We divide this by 5 (the number of samples) to get the average of 51.8. Do this for each of the columns.

Step Three

Calculate the range (R) by taking the largest number in the column (in Jan it was 61) and subtracting the smallest number in the column (in Jan it was 45). The result is the range (or 16 for Jan). Do this for the other columns.

Step Four

Put the number of samples in each column right under the range.

Step Five

Calculate the average of the averages. Now this may sound a little silly, but it is necessary for the control chart. Just add up the averages (51.8, 53.4, 53.2, 49.4, 54.2, and

Step Five

Calculate the average of the averages. Now this may sound a little silly, but it is necessary for the control chart. Just add up the averages (51.8, 53.4, 53.2, 49.4, 54.2, and 51.4). This total for our observations is 313.4. Divide this by the number of columns. In our case, we have six columns so the average of the averages is 313.4, divided by 6, or 52.2333. The sign we use for the average of the averages is $\bar{\bar{X}}$, so we have the following:

$$\bar{\bar{X}} = 52.2333$$

Step Six

Calculate the average of the ranges. In our example we have the following ranges:

16, 10, 9, 5, 14, and 7

These total 61. Divide this by the number of columns. In our case, we have six columns so the average of the ranges is 61, divided by 6, or 10.1667. The sign we use for the average of the ranges is $\bar{R}$, so we have the following:

$$\bar{R} = 10.1667$$

We will now use both of these numbers to develop our control chart.

Step Seven

Before we continue we need to incorporate the statistical chart we mentioned earlier, the Table of Factors. Without this chart we could go no further in our development of a control chart.

Table of Factors			
Number of Observations in Subgroup (n)	Factors for X Chart	Factors for R Chart	
	A2	D3	D4
2	1.880	0	3.268
3	1.023	0	2.574
4	0.729	0	2.282
5	0.577	0	2.114
6	0.483	0	2.004
7	0.419	0.076	1.924
8	0.373	0.136	1.864
9	0.337	0.184	1.816
10	0.308	0.223	1.777

Now we are able to calculate the Upper Control Limits (UCL) and Lower Control Limits (LCL) for the mean and the range using the results we obtained earlier (Step Five and Step Six) and the data from the Table of Factors above.

The Mean

UCL (Mean) $= \bar{\bar{X}} + (A2 \cdot \bar{R})$
$= 52.233 + (0.577 \cdot 10.167)$
$= 52.233 + 5.897$
$= 58.130$

LCL (Mean) $= \bar{\bar{X}} - (A2 \cdot \bar{R})$
$= 52.233 - (0.577 \cdot 10.16)$
$= 52.233 - 5.897$
$= 46.336$

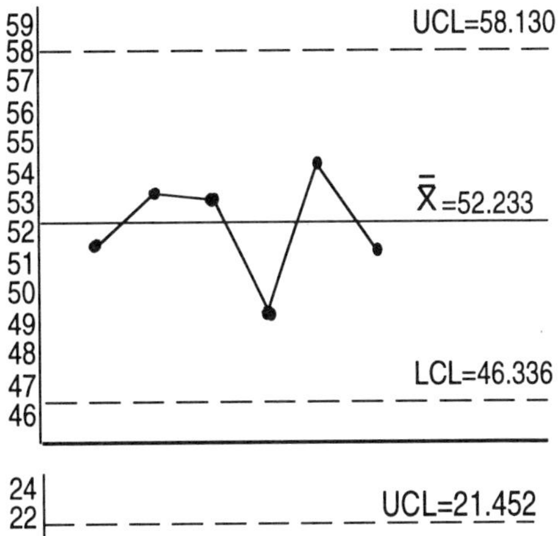

The Range

UCL (Range) $= D4 \cdot \bar{R}$
$= 2.11 \cdot 10.167$
$= 21.452$

LCL (Range) $= D3 \cdot \bar{R}$
$= 0 \cdot 10.167$
$= 0$

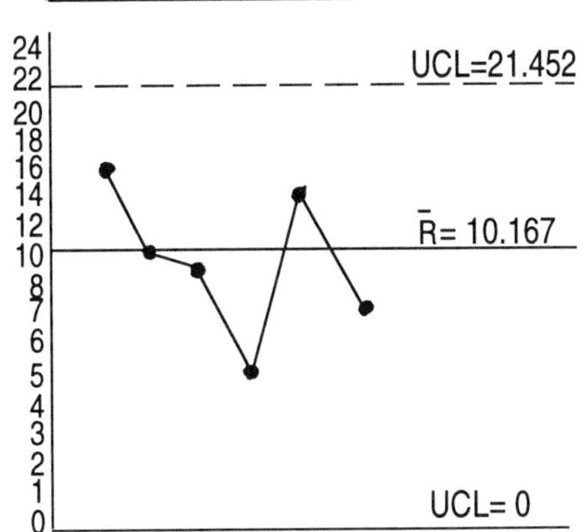

As a result of all this work, what do we know about our data? Are we in control? We'll find out by examining our original data:

	Jan	Feb	Mar	Apr	May	Jun
Number of Days	52	55	54	51	46	49
	46	47	48	50	60	53
	45	57	53	47	57	47
	61	55	54	52	51	54
	55	53	57	47	57	54
Average ($\bar{X}$)	51.8	53.4	53.2	49.4	54.2	51.4
Range (R)	16	10	9	5	14	7
Number of Samples	5	5	5	5	5	5

Study the two control charts that we have developed (one for the mean and the other for the range). Look at the individual points plotted for the mean (average) in the first chart. Notice that not one value, representing the average, falls either above the Upper Control Limit (58.130) or below the Lower Control Limit (46.336). Therefore, This process is in control.

The second control chart for the range also shows the process to be in control. No values calculated for this chart fall above the Upper Control Limit or fall below the Lower Control Limit.

GENERAL GUIDELINES

- A process is considered **out of control** *if one or more of the data points (averages or ranges) falls outside the control limits.*
- A process is considered **out of control** *if the data contains unpredictable values, trends, or cycles* (e.g., if there are two points out of three very close to the Upper Control Limit or to the Lower Control Limit).
- A process is considered **out of control** *if there are nine or more data points falling in succession either above or below the mean.*
- If a process is **out of control**, ask if there has been a change in policy, personnel, budget, or reporting.

BLUE CHIPS

- Later, we will be discussing **run charts**, which are much easier to construct than are control charts. The run chart merely tracks data over a specific period of time and allows the team to spot patterns or trends. The control chart goes beyond this and helps the team not only spot trends, but provides a statistically sound Upper Control Limit and Lower Control Limit. This additional input permits the team to see if the variations in the data are just usual variations inherent in any process, or if something very unusual is happening because of some special factor. Unusual deviations occur when the process is out of control.
- Of all the tools we present in this workbook, the control chart is the one that may require consulting an expert on in your agency. It is complex, and a statistician can help with not only the development of the chart, but what data should be collected.
- Teams, using the control chart, can not only address the special unknown causes of the variation, but also elements that cause variation even when the process is in control. It is unlikely that all variation will be eliminated, but as the process is refined and improved, less variation will be found.
- When the special causes are eliminated, and the process is in control, the team may elect to move on to another component of the process or a different process. It would not hurt to periodically construct a control chart to determine if the process ever does go out of control again.

Question: If nature used a control chart, would we be here?

7 CUSTOMER SURVEYS

Because the customer is the focus and the heart of all that we do in our efforts to improve processes, everyone involved in process improvement should remember the following acronym:

Customer satisfaction increased by

All associates involved, working in

Teams, to improve processes in

Small, incremental steps

In government, customers are called by a variety of names, including "clients" and "consumers." Some have objected to calling those we serve "customers," somehow feeling that the word is a negative one. However, Joseph Juran sees the term as neutral and defines a customer as "someone who is *impacted by the product.*" In government, that "product" consists of services offered.

Customers are not always just the people who walk in the front door. Actually, given Juran's definition, we are all customers of someone within our own agency. We are "internal" customers for we are impacted by the services others offer us. When we submit our request for travel reimbursement, we are customers of the travel section. When we decide to purchase a new desk, we are customers of the purchasing section. Their job is to increase our satisfaction and for us to feel good about the interaction.

We have found that most customers essentially want the same from government as they would from any company in the private sector—friendly service, flexibility, problem resolution, and recovery if necessary. Factors that are often mentioned as important to customers also include timeliness, consistency and integrity. One problem often faced by a team is that they do not know what customers really want or what is important to them. That is where the customer survey can be helpful.

WHAT IS IT?

The **Customer Survey** is a tool to increase an understanding of who your customers are, what they consider important, what they want from you, and what they think of you. What the survey accomplishes depends upon what the team wants to find out. As a result of what is learned, it is possible to improve processes so that customer satisfaction is increased.

WHY SHOULD IT BE USED?

The customer survey can be the most helpful instrument to give the team an understanding of what the customer's demands, requirements and standards are. The importance of surveys is demonstrated in how very popular the "polls" have become to individuals seeking public office. Those surveys help the candidates understand what the electorate considers important and what they want done. In government, improvements based upon sound surveys pay dividends by increasing satisfaction in areas considered important by the customer.

WHAT DOES A TEAM NEED TO USE IT?

Volumes have been written about customer surveys, proper polling practices, and validity of results. There is no need for graduate study to develop a good survey. What is needed is a desire to discover what is important to your customers, and how they feel about services. Use your own experience. You know what is important to you. Putting yourself in your customer's place is a very good beginning. To construct a survey, follow the steps outlined below.

HOW DO WE DO IT ? WHAT ARE THE RULES?

Step One

Put yourself in your customer's shoes. If you were the customer walking into your office what would you expect? Would you want to see a long waiting line? What about the looks of the building? Are the chairs comfortable? Are the bathrooms clean? Is the parking lot convenient and safe? Think about the kinds of questions a customer might ask.

Step Two

Decide whether you are going to use a printed survey alone, a printed survey with an interview, or just an interview. Each has its place in obtaining information, however, we will concentrate on the written survey here.

Step Three

Design a draft survey form. Keep it simple. Decide if it will be a "confidential" one without signatures. There are benefits to both signed and unsigned surveys. A confidential survey may provide better results (more accurate perceptions by the customer), for there will be less fear of retaliation. A survey that is signed would let you contact the customer for additional information or clarification.

Step Four

Do a pilot with the draft form. See what results you obtain, and modify as necessary.

Step Five

Conduct the survey.

Step Six

Analyze the results of the survey. Are the results what you expected? Where were the surprises, if any. Can the data suggest improvements for the team to address? Are there any suggestions that can be forwarded to management for resolution?

Step Seven

Survey again. Keep the surveys coming in while the team continues its work. You may wish to change some of the questions, but always keep your hands on the pulse of what your customers want.

EXAMPLES

We present the following *actual* surveys prepared by teams working in government. Understand that no survey is perfect, and your team may do even better! (Because these samples are all in the public domain, they may be copied.)

Bureau of Claims and Benefits
Claims Operations
Survey of Benefits Quality Control Unit

Date____________
Local Office ________________________
CC# _____

We are attempting to evaluate our performance and would appreciate your input. Please take a few minutes to answer the following questions and return the survey to Claims Operation, Room 208 Caldwell Building, Tallahassee, Florida 32399-0244

Please rate the quality of service by circling the appropriate response and providing any written comments which you believe would be helpful.

5 = Very Good 4 = Good 3 = Average 2 = Poor 1 = Unsatisfactory

1. How would you rate the overall service provided to you by this local claims office?

   5 4 3 2 1 Comment:

2. When contacting this claims office, are your concerns handled in a competent manner?

   5 4 3 2 1 Comment:

3. Do you feel the staff members assisting you were knowledgeable and well-trained?

   5 4 3 2 1 Comment:

4. How would you rate the courtesy shown during your contact with this office?

   5 4 3 2 1 Comment

5. How would you rate the office's response time to your requests?

   5 4 3 2 1 Comment

6. How do you rate the quality of work received from this local office?

   5 4 3 2 1 Comment

7. Is local office training needed? If so, what type?

8. What can we do to improve local office service?

The Division of Vocational Rehabilitation used the following Satisfaction Interview to assess how their customers were feeling about services. This form was used by specially trained interviewers who met with customers throughout the state.

SATISFACTION INTERVIEW

1. Has your counselor explained why you are eligible for the Vocational Rehabilitation Program?

2. Has your counselor listened to your ideas and suggestions about your Individualized Written Rehabilitation Program?

3. Has your counselor explained to you what actions you can take if you are not happy with services (your rights)?

4. Have services been provided within a reasonable time frame?

5. Has your counselor been available to you when needed?

6. Would you refer a friend to vocational rehabilitation?

7. Were you treated courteously by your counselor and other staff from vocational rehabilitation?

8. Is there anything else you would like to tell us about your experience with vocational rehabilitation?

The Division of Unemployment Compensation, Bureau of Tax in the Florida Department of Labor and Employment Security used the following letter to see what employers thought of the services offered by the Division's telephones.

RE: Telephone Service
ACCOUNT #: __________

Dear Employer:

A review of our records reveals that you made a telephone call to our Tax Rates Unit in Tallahassee, Florida recently. In a continuing effort to improve the quality of our services, we would appreciate any comments or suggestions you may have. We hope you will take the time to complete this survey by grading each category on a scale from one to five (poor to excellent). In addition, a place has been provided for your comments and suggestions:

1. Was our representative	Poor 1	Fair 2	Good 3	Very Good 4	Excellent 5
a. polite/courteous?	____	____	_____	_______	_______
b. informative/knowledgeable	____	____	_____	_______	_______
c. concerned/helpful?	____	____	_____	_______	_______
2. Was the information you received					
a. accurate/correct?	____	____	_____	_______	_______
b. thorough/complete?	____	____	_____	_______	_______
c. clear/concise?	____	____	_____	_______	_______

3. With whom did you speak? ____________________
(optional)

4. Would you like to speak with this representative in the future should you have to call again?
______Yes _________No

5. How many times were you transferred before you reached the appropriate representative?

____

6. Comments and/or suggestions:

____

____

Internal customers in the Bureau of Appeals were given the opportunity to provide feedback with the following questionnaire.

Bureau of Appeals

This questionnaire is designed to help evaluate perceived problems in the Bureau of Appeals. Your input is very important in assisting in prioritizing these problems and developing possible solutions.

Please respond by checking the appropriate block indicating the degree to which you feel each item is a problem. Space is provided for additional problem areas not listed. For field offices, it is especially important that you list any additional concerns which are unique to your location. Space is also provided for you to suggest what you can do personally to improve overall working situations and/or what others should do to resolve these problems.

CURRENT JOB CLASSIFICATION: ______________________________

SA = Strongly Agree A = Agree NA = Not a Problem D = Disagree SD = Strongly Disagree

	SA	A	NA	D	SD
1. Associates within this office are aware of the standards expected by the supervisor.					
2. Associates within this office are given opportunities to improve their skills through training.					
3. The supervisor supports and encourages new methods and techniques.					
4. The supervisor cares about associates in this office as people as well as professionals.					
5. Associates in this office perform as a team.					
6. Decisions about work assignments are made without involving the associates in this office.					
7. The atmosphere in this office encourages problem solving.					
8. Innovation is not seen as necessary in this office.					
9. Associates in this office can influence decisions made within the total organization.					
10. The supervisor tries to improve our office working conditions.					
11. It is a pleasure to work in this office.					
12. Associates in this office are used effectively.					
13. In this office power is primarily reserved for the supervisor.					
14. The supervisor acknowledges good performance.					
15. Associates in this office are frustrated by a lack of direction from the supervisor.					
16. Associates are encouraged to participate in formulating objectives for the office.					
17. The supervisor has the ability to perceive potential problems.					
18. Associates in this office feel an allegiance to each other.					
19. There is little team work within this office.					
20. Associates understand the relationship between their job assignments and the Bureau's mission.					
21. The supervisor strives to meet office needs and those of the associates.					
22. The supervisor shows favoritism towards some members of the office.					
23. The associates of this office do not need constant supervision in order to work well together.					
24. Associates have the power to influence the direction of change in this office.					
25. There is good communication in this office concerning changes.					
26. Associates have little input in setting office objectives.					
27. In discussions, the supervisor listens to the associates' ideas.					

Please use the back for problems not listed, suggestions to resolve these problems or for additional comments.

8 DEMING CYCLE

A few pages back, we discussed the **Cause and Effect** diagram, but did not mention that it is also known as the "Ishikawa" diagram. That is the name of the Japanese scientist who first described the diagram and popularized its use. Thus, we have at least three names for the tool—the cause and effect diagram, the Ishikawa diagram and the "fish-bone" diagram.

The same is true for the **Deming Cycle**. Actually Dr. Deming gave credit to Walter Shewhart, who probably originated the concept. For years, reference was made to the "Shewhart Cycle." Now we often see it called the **Plan, Do, Check, Act** cycle or tool. You may still see it called the Shewhart Cycle or the Deming Cycle. In honor of Dr. Deming we will call it the Deming Cycle.

WHAT IS IT?

The best way to describe the cycle is through the use of a graphic. The cycle flows clockwise through the following steps: Plan, Do, Check, Act. This is the process that teams use as they study the process, develop a plan, implement a pilot, check results, and act in full scale implementation.

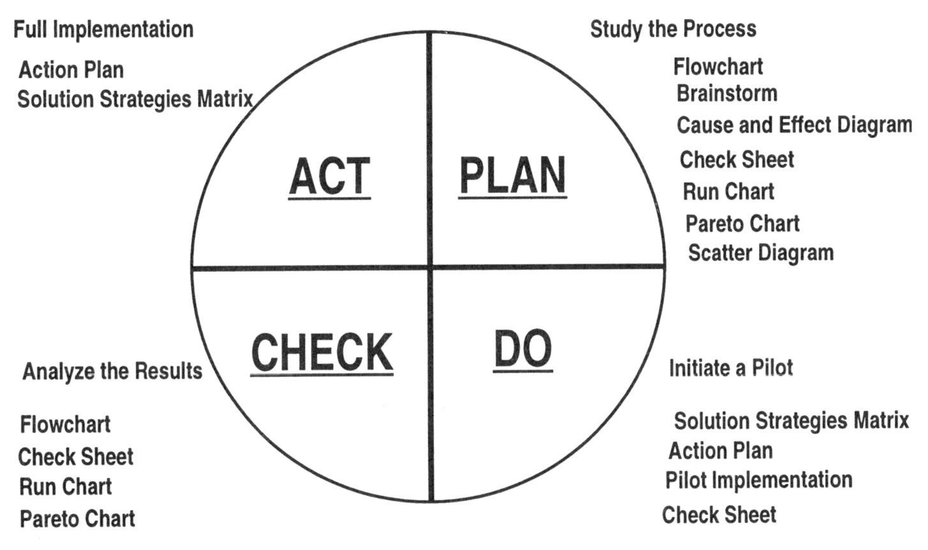

The tools listed are suggested tools—others may be used.

WHY DO WE DO IT?

The Deming Cycle is a great tool to help the team organize their thoughts and action. Too often, it is relatively easy for a team to lose its way. This is especially true in the early stages of team work when team members are unfamiliar with quality improvement techniques. Although it appears almost too simple, the Deming Cycle is a handy tool to come back to when teams begin to falter.

WHAT DOES A TEAM NEED TO USE IT?

Dr. Deming often used a table napkin to explain the cycle to his students. A pencil would also be handy. Although one is tempted to say "this isn't rocket science," do not be fooled by its simplicity. It is a powerful technique.

HOW DO WE DO IT? WHAT ARE THE RULES?

Understand the Deming Cycle. Note that a key concept of the cycle is that it never ends. Once you have completed one revolution and are finishing the "Act" quadrant, you move right back into the "Plan" quadrant to start all over. This is in keeping with Dr. Deming's Fifth Point:

> Constantly locate problems. Improve constantly and forever the system of production and service, to improve quality and productivity, and thus constantly reduce costs.

Begin the cycle by following the sequence below.

Step One

Draw a circle. Divide the circle into four quadrants. Label these four quadrants "Plan," "Do," "Check," and "Act."

Step Two

Think about what needs to be done in the first quadrant—Plan. If this is a "brand-new" cycle, you *may spend a lot of time* in this first quadrant. This is expected. If the team is just beginning, they will want to ensure that they have already

- established a *mission* for the team,
- developed *values* for the team,
- selected a *process* to study and improve, and
- discussed their *needs* for training and information.

If the above steps have not been taken, they could be considered a part of the first quadrant. The team begins planning for change by flowcharting their process, brainstorming possible causes for problems, collecting data, and finally analyzing the data. During this process, the team may find that they do not have all the skills and understandings necessary and may call upon assistance from their process improvement guides.

Step Three

With the analysis of data complete, the team may wish to make use of the Solution Strategies Matrix to select possible actions. With the best alternative selected, the team develops an action plan and implements a small pilot project to observe results. This is where mistakes can be made without costing a great deal of time or money.

Step Four

The team checks its results in the third quadrant. Have customers noticed the improvements made? Are the waiting lines shorter? Do the internal customers notice any change? Do people appear a little happier? What do the statistics show? Has the Pareto chart changed from when it was first constructed with the earlier data? What worked? What failed to make a difference? Have improvements been made? Does the team need additional assistance from management?

Step Five

With the results of the third quadrant, the team moves forward in the Act quadrant by implementing the good changes made in the first three quadrants. This is the place where full implementation is accomplished.

Perhaps this all sounds very similar to other "wheels" of problem-solving. It is. We mentioned earlier that this concept was first popularized by Walter Shewhart. But there are others very similar. A "six-spoke" problem solving wheel looks like this:

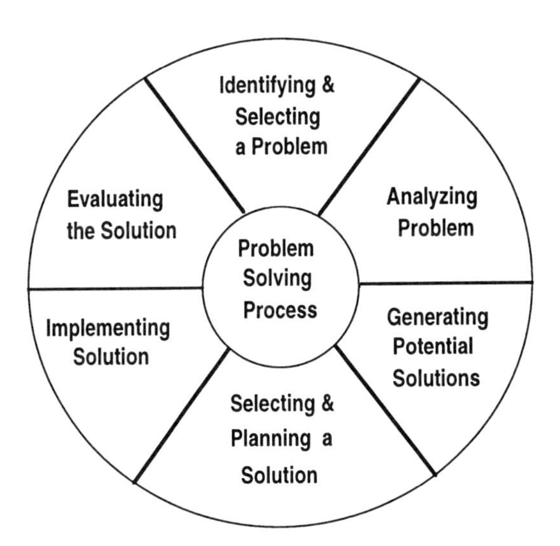

EXAMPLE

We previously mentioned in ***Step Two*** assistance available from a "process improvement guide." Such guides were selected in the Department of Labor and Employment Security to:

> "...provide technical assistance to quality improvement teams as an outside consultant, their job is to help team members in the group process by observing and evaluating how the team functions; they also provide training as needed in quality improvement tools, team dynamics, the teachings of the

quality gurus, including Dr. Deming, and help the teams prepare presentations to the quality council."

The quality improvement guides used the Deming Cycle to map their strategies to meet this assignment. The following, taken from their notes, parallel the Deming Cycle:

Plan

- Communicate with agency leaders, especially the ones who will empower you in a particular team.
- Develop awareness of process improvement needs among leaders.
- Team leader and team facilitator jointly plan early meetings carefully; study how to conduct successful meetings.
- Plan for inputting data to statewide team tracking system.
- Develop plan for particular roles and how to select individuals.
- Have knowledge of process improvement steps.
- Develop process improvement supports: (1) values, (2) vision, (3) mission, and (4) goals.
- Keep sharp focus: Study Deming's fourteen points; watch and discuss videos on how to conduct successful meetings.
- Analyze process, using TQM goals.
- Flowchart (get large picture first, then refine to more detail later).
- Identify measuring points.
- Benchmark with data collected; use checklist if needed.
- Use cause and effect diagram.
- Use Pareto chart.
- Choose solution; identify elements of process change.
- Modify flowchart.

Do

- Apply solutions; put process improvements to work.
- Use control chart; narrow the variation.

Check

- Monitor changes.
- Get feedback.
- Communicate with suppliers and customers.

Act

- Make personnel adjustments if necessary.
- Write policy revisions based upon the changes.
- Modify agency procedures and/or rules based upon changes.

9 FLOWCHARTS

If there is one tool or technique that stands above all in the tool box of quality tools, it is without a doubt the **Flowchart**. In our minds, it is nearly impossible to discuss quality improvements in a process without understanding the process with a flowchart.

WHAT IS IT?

A **Flowchart** is a graphic representation of the flow of work. It is a map of what occurs. There are several kinds of flowcharts; however, one type is most often used and will be referred to in this workbook as "flowchart." The others include "top-down flowchart," "work-flow diagram," and "responsibilities work chart."

WHY SHOULD IT BE USED?

The flowchart shows the order of work, what takes place, and even who is doing it at times. It is a common reference that all team members can examine to understand the process. It is a picture that all can agree upon which can be shared with others not on the team. The flowchart is an outstanding tool to share with associates new to the organization, for they can then readily see what actually takes place in a process.

WHAT DOES A TEAM NEED TO USE IT?

A basic understanding of the differences in the four types of "flowcharts," and a working understanding of some of the symbols used in flowcharting are required. The following discussion centers on this understanding.

WHAT ARE THE MAJOR DIFFERENCES IN THE FOUR TYPES OF FLOW-CHARTS?

The four charts meet different needs, which will soon become apparent after examples are provided for each.

1. **"Top-down flowchart."** This is a flowchart that shows only the major steps in a process. The details are purposely eliminated for a very special reason. Many steps develop in a process merely because someone, often a supervisor or a manager, felt that the step was absolutely necessary. Perhaps a problem developed in the process that was cured by this little extra step. Maybe someone thought that a rule required the step. Maybe a federal law requiring it was later repealed, but the step remained. The top-down flowchart shows just what is essential without steps detailing inspections, audits or required approvals.

2. **"Flowchart."** This is the flowchart that we will concentrate on in this workbook. This flowchart shows sufficient detail to enable the team to understand where problems may be developing, where there are "loops" that should be examined, where customers may be having to wait for an approval, etc. This flowchart makes use of the symbols ordinarily associated with flowcharts.
3. **"Work-flow diagram."** The "work-flow diagram" is not often used by teams examining processes in government. This is unfortunate, for the diagram has real potential to improve processes. This tool uses diagrams of the movements of people, materials or information. It can show very graphically where problems exist. For example, a work-flow diagram would show the movements of a customer trying to find the right office to apply for an unemployment check.
4. **"Responsibilities work chart."** The "responsibilities work chart" takes the flowchart one step further by outlining not only the steps involved, but who is going to assume responsibility for each step. This would be an outstanding chart for a family planning a dinner party or a wedding. It is also very useful for a project team so that there is no confusion as to who is responsible for various phases of project completion. In this respect, it can resemble diagrams used by project management software.

HOW DO WE DO IT? WHAT ARE THE RULES?

Follow the next sequence to learn how to design each type of flowchart.

TOP-DOWN FLOWCHART

Recall that a top-down flowchart shows only the major steps in a process. It eliminates the details found in other flowcharts and concentrates on the "big picture." Below is an example of a top-down that illustrates the **Vocational Rehabilitation Process.**

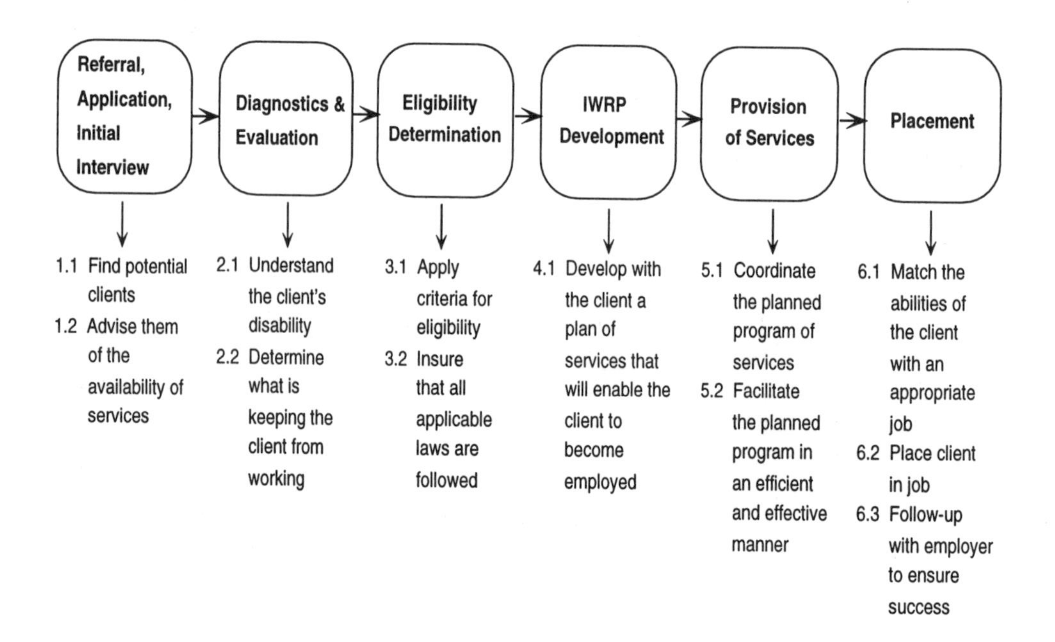

FLOWCHART

This is the flowchart that most of us are familiar with, which makes use of the symbols usually associated with flowcharts. The other day we saw a team preparing a flowchart with a template that had symbols for the following:

Process	Input/Output	Manual Operation	Off page Connector
Preparation	Merge	Decision	Magnetic Tape
Display	Auxiliary Operation	Connector	Manual Input
Extract	Communications	Terminal Interrupt	Punched Card
Keying	Punched Tape	On-line Storage	Transmittal Tape
Document			

The flowcharting template was one developed by IBM for use in showing the flow of a process concerned with computer data.

We do not recommend that teams use all the symbols available on this template. Many are inappropriate. Teams can get bogged down in arguments over what kind of box to draw and lose sight of the purpose for the flowchart.

The basics:

- A process is a series of steps that is performed to produce a product or service.
- A flowchart graphically represents the flow of work (processes).
- A flowchart may show where there are delays, problems, "loops," or omissions.
- A flowchart may be used to document the "actual" way a process works, vs. the "official" way it is supposed to work, vs. a possible improved way.
- People performing the work and who are therefore closest to the work are the best people to flowchart the process.

Tips

- Use common sense.
- Flowcharts are never final; they are fluid and often change.
- Do not worry about which "boxes" to use. Feel free to make up your own symbols. Use whatever works with your team. You might end up using only rectangles and diamonds.
- Get the entire team involved in the flowcharting. Do not let one person, because of rank or stature, influence the team's analysis of the process.
- Try using large sheets of paper posted on the wall for all to see. Consider placing the draft efforts in a hallway, or next to the break room where others who are not team members can view the process.
- Even if the process is working now does not mean that it cannot be improved.

Questions to Ask

- Are there any "loops?" Why?
- Does each step add value? Could a step, or steps, be eliminated?
- Where are the delays? Why?
- Where are measurements taken? Why?
- Where should the measurements be taken? Why?
- Where do customer complaints originate? How do we know?
- Where do most of the errors occur? Who finds out?
- Where are workers identifying problems with the process? Do they have suggestions for improvement?
- How can the process be improved?

EXAMPLES

The following examples are *real* flowcharts produced by teams in a government agency. While they may not be perfect, they represent the best thinking of team members who were working on the improvement of a process. The first was prepared by a team studying the flow of mail in a headquarters office.

Distribution of Mail

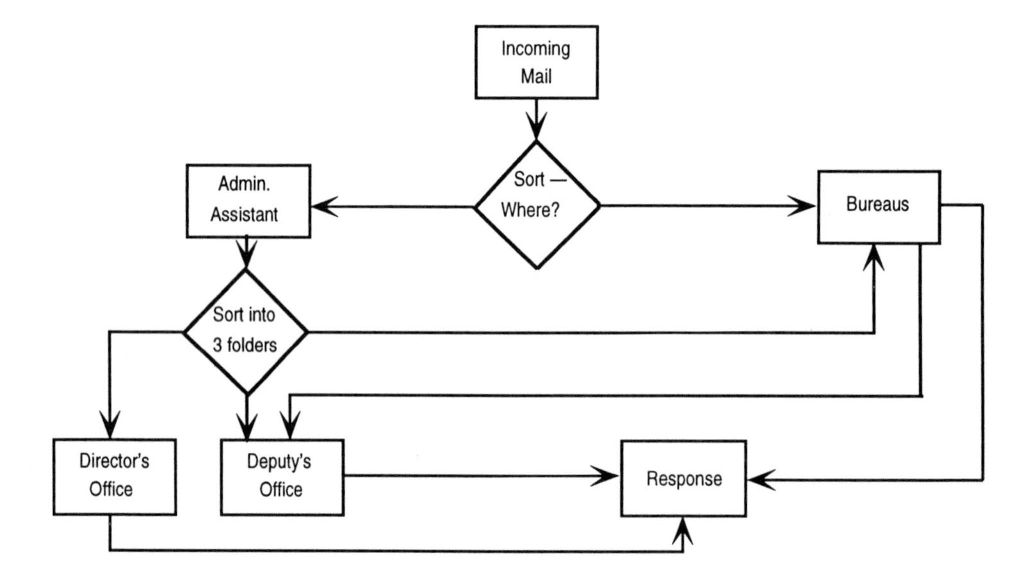

FLOW CHART SYMBOLS

Note that the team preparing the "Distribution of Mail" used only three symbols—the rectangle, the diamond and flow lines. We have found that the majority of teams find these symbols to be most helpful. In fact, the following symbols account for over 95% of those used in flowcharts in a two-year period in the Department of Labor and Security.

The rectangle box is probably the most frequently used symbol. The box designates an activity when something happens, when something is changed or arranged for the next step, or when planning or analysis takes place. A brief statement of the activity is contained within the rectangle.

The diamond is perhaps the second most frequently used symbol. This represents a decision point from which two or more paths can be taken. It is often a question that can be answered "yes" or "no." The path taken depends upon the answer to the question. Note that the path identifies the answer.

This symbol can be used to identify a termination point (either the beginning or end of a process). It is helpful to include the description within the symbol ("start," "begin," "stop," and "end.").

The document symbol identifies a document that is essential to the process, or one that is produced by the process (that the team may find less essential).

Flow lines identify the path the process takes, with the arrowhead showing direction.

The connector is used to provide transition from one page to another when the flow chart is too long for one page. It is helpful to direct the reader to another flowchart for an entirely different process.

EXAMPLES

The following pages will contain a few examples of flowcharts developed by actual teams. To begin, however, a light-hearted flowchart appears on the next page to show that almost anything can be examined with a flowchart.

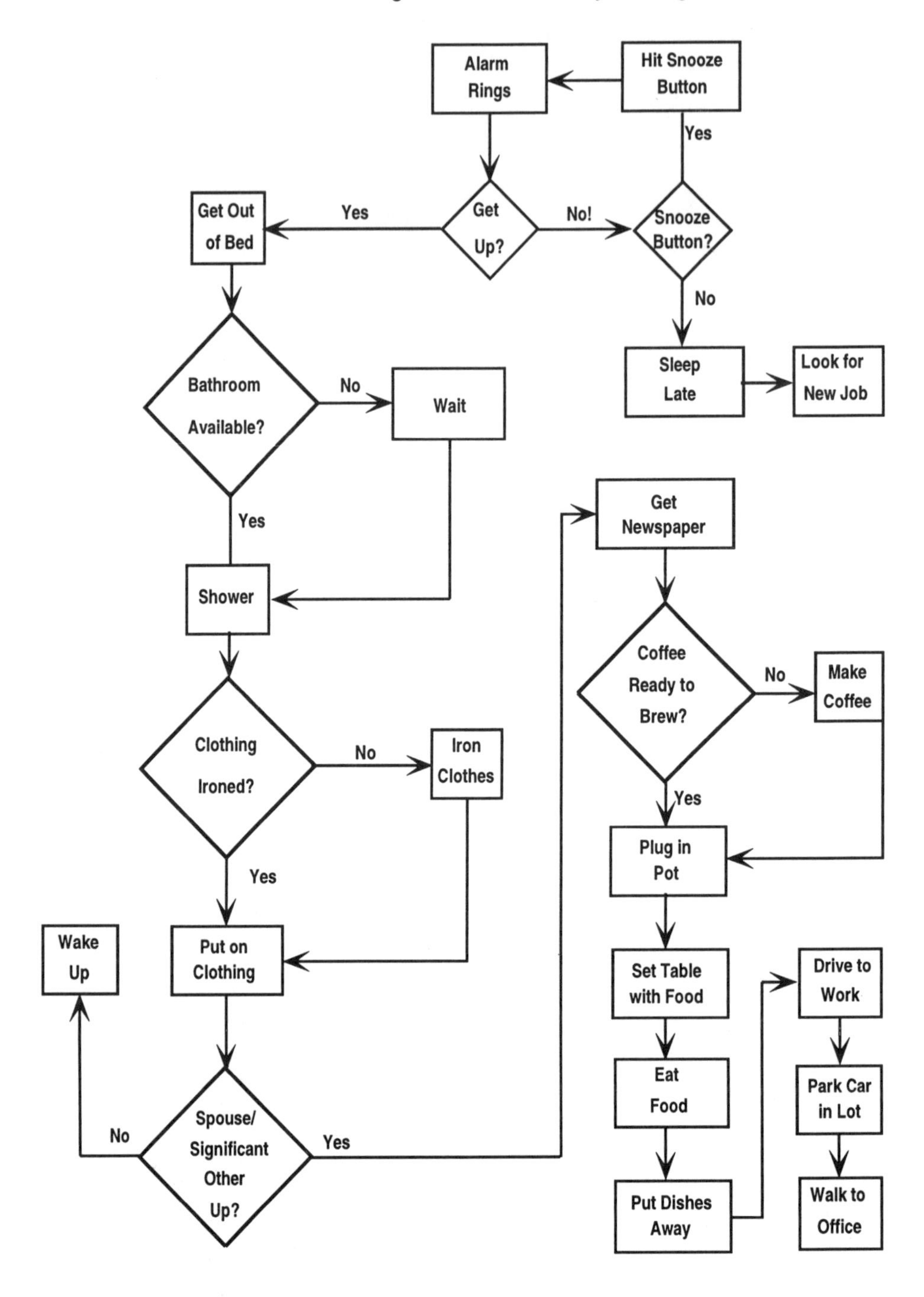

Getting to Work on a Monday Morning
Alarm Rings
Hit Snooze Button
Yes
Get Out of Bed
Yes
Get Up?
No!
Snooze Button?
No
Sleep Late
Look for New Job
Bathroom Available?
No
Wait
Yes
Get Newspaper
Shower
Coffee Ready to Brew?
No
Make Coffee
Clothing Ironed?
No
Iron Clothes
Yes
Plug in Pot
Yes
Wake Up
Put on Clothing
Set Table with Food
Drive to Work
Eat Food
Park Car in Lot
No
Spouse/ Significant Other Up?
Yes
Put Dishes Away
Walk to Office

EXAMPLE

Teams should not be overly concerned with the "boxes" when they begin flowcharting. The example below makes use of a few unconventional symbols that do not appear in any books we've read. Nevertheless, *the team knew* what they were talking about—and that is all that matters.

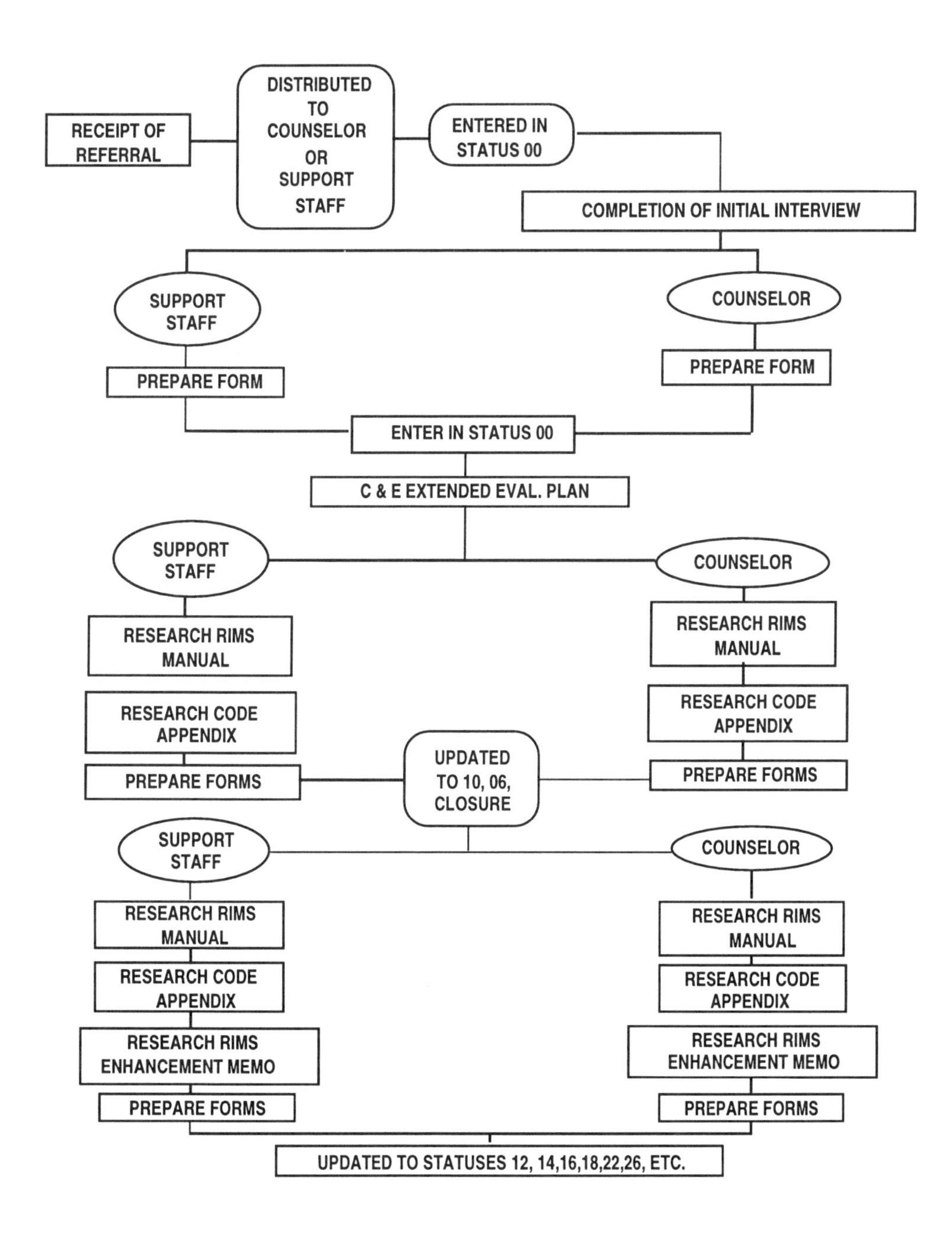

EXAMPLE

The following pages contain additional examples of flowcharts prepared by teams in the Department of Labor and Employment Security. The first is one developed by a team studying the lease process, *prior* to the implementation of improvements recommended by the team. It is easy to see why it took so long to get a lease through the system. Note the use of connectors to direct the reader to the next page.

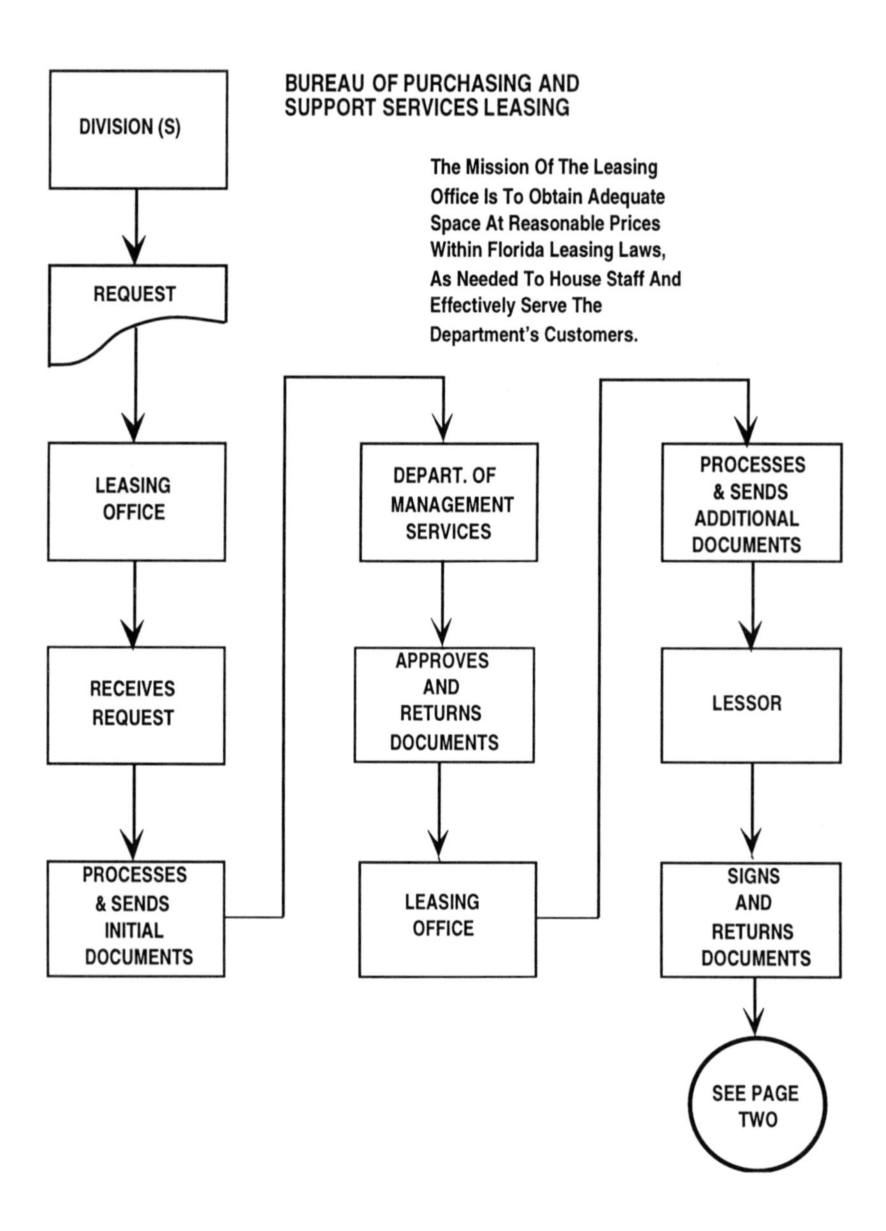

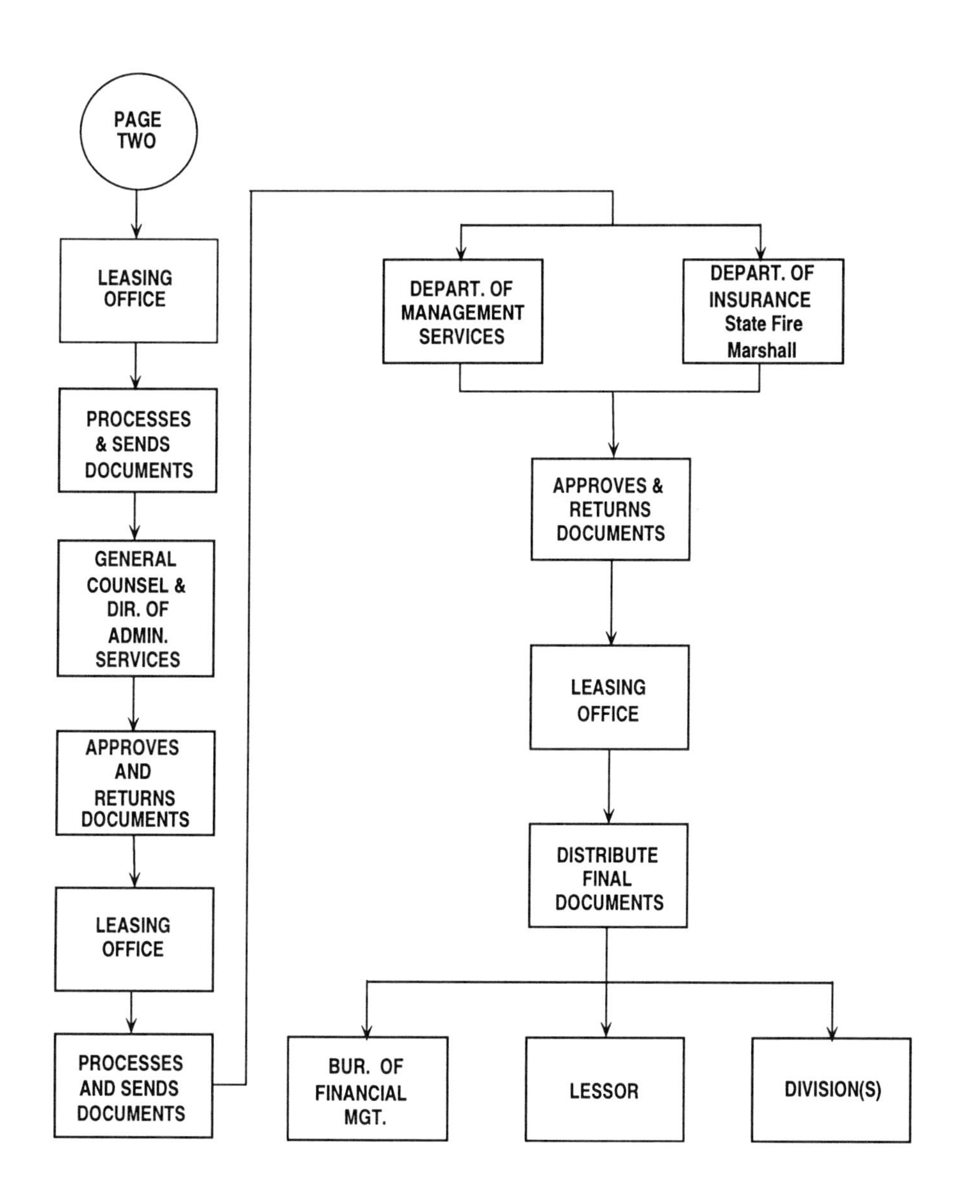
PAGE TWO
LEASING OFFICE
PROCESSES & SENDS DOCUMENTS
GENERAL COUNSEL & DIR. OF ADMIN. SERVICES
APPROVES AND RETURNS DOCUMENTS
LEASING OFFICE
PROCESSES AND SENDS DOCUMENTS
DEPART. OF MANAGEMENT SERVICES
DEPART. OF INSURANCE State Fire Marshall
APPROVES & RETURNS DOCUMENTS
LEASING OFFICE
DISTRIBUTE FINAL DOCUMENTS
BUR. OF FINANCIAL MGT.
LESSOR
DIVISION(S)

WHERE IS MY TRAVEL CHECK?

This is a question that was heard many times in state agencies. Unfortunately, the bureaucracy apparently thrives on any process that involves money. Add to this the possibility for misuse and fraud, and a nightmare of audit checks and reviews occurs. Shown below is the process a team discovered as they began making improvements.

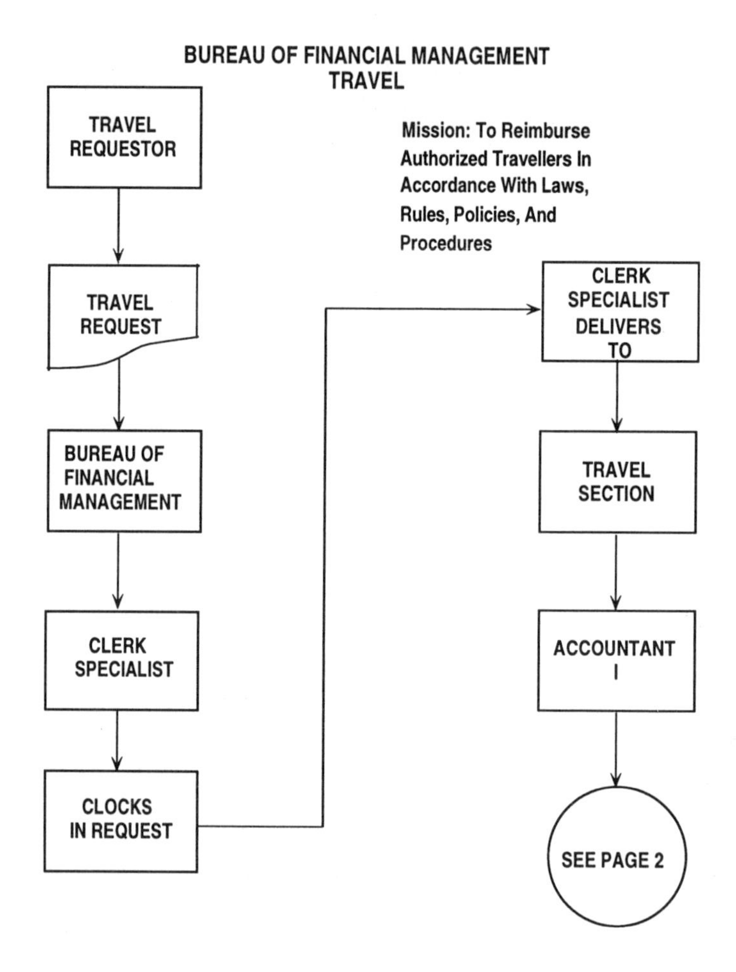

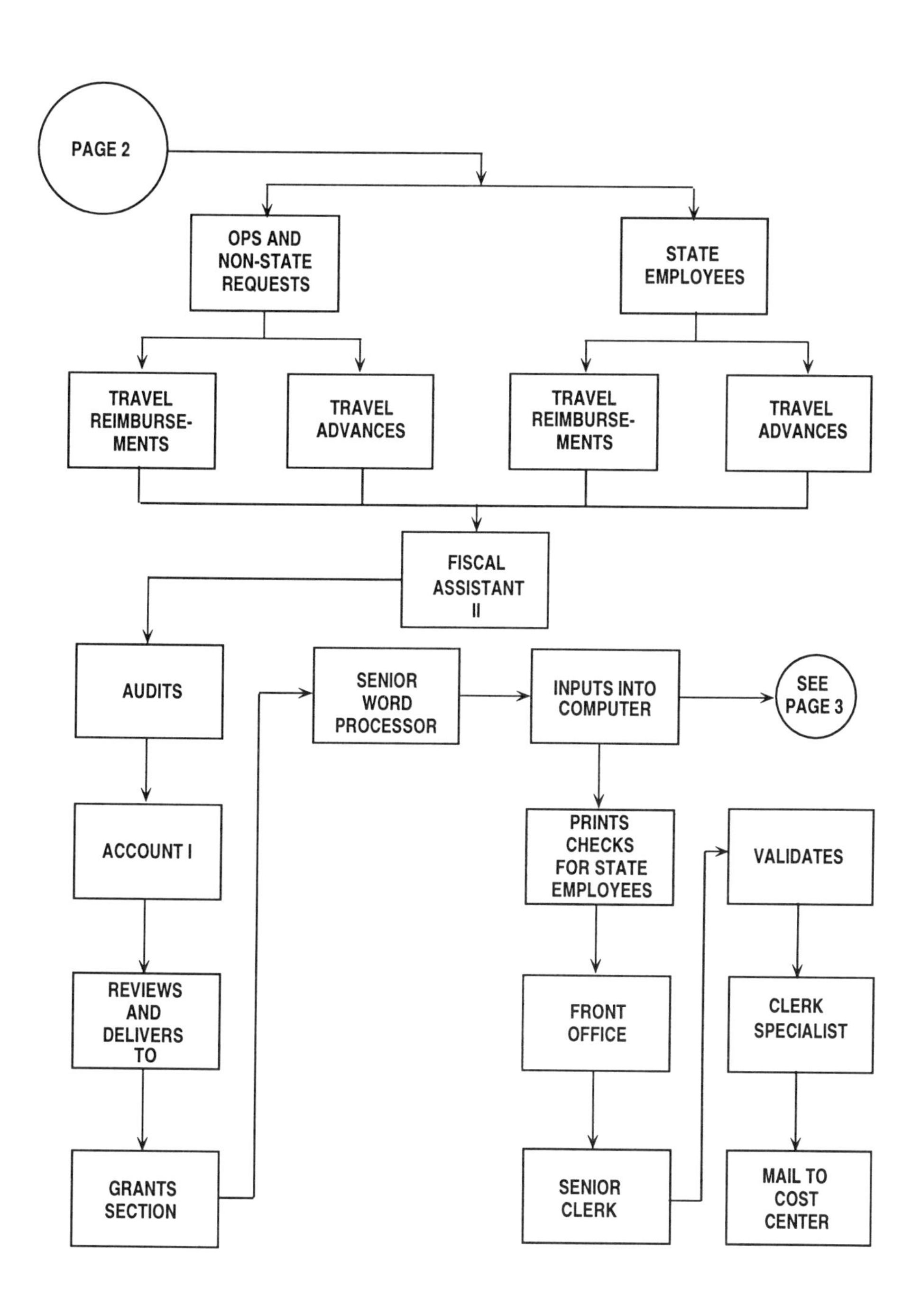
PAGE 2
OPS AND NON-STATE REQUESTS
STATE EMPLOYEES
TRAVEL REIMBURSE-MENTS
TRAVEL ADVANCES
TRAVEL REIMBURSE-MENTS
TRAVEL ADVANCES
FISCAL ASSISTANT II
AUDITS
SENIOR WORD PROCESSOR
INPUTS INTO COMPUTER
SEE PAGE 3
ACCOUNT I
PRINTS CHECKS FOR STATE EMPLOYEES
VALIDATES
REVIEWS AND DELIVERS TO
FRONT OFFICE
CLERK SPECIALIST
GRANTS SECTION
SENIOR CLERK
MAIL TO COST CENTER

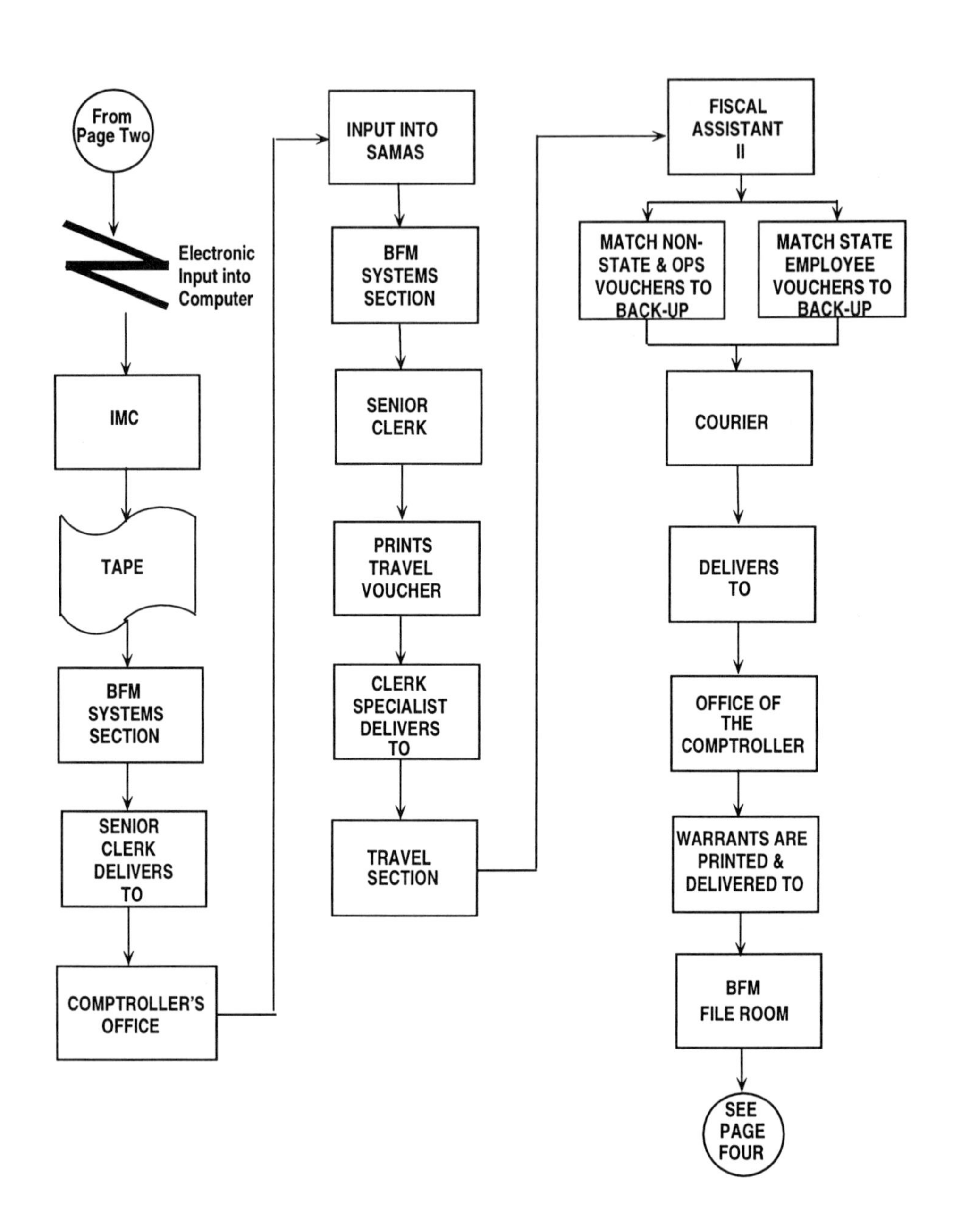
From Page Two
Electronic Input into Computer
IMC
TAPE
BFM SYSTEMS SECTION
SENIOR CLERK DELIVERS TO
COMPTROLLER'S OFFICE
INPUT INTO SAMAS
BFM SYSTEMS SECTION
SENIOR CLERK
PRINTS TRAVEL VOUCHER
CLERK SPECIALIST DELIVERS TO
TRAVEL SECTION
FISCAL ASSISTANT II
MATCH NON-STATE & OPS VOUCHERS TO BACK-UP
MATCH STATE EMPLOYEE VOUCHERS TO BACK-UP
COURIER
DELIVERS TO
OFFICE OF THE COMPTROLLER
WARRANTS ARE PRINTED & DELIVERED TO
BFM FILE ROOM
SEE PAGE FOUR

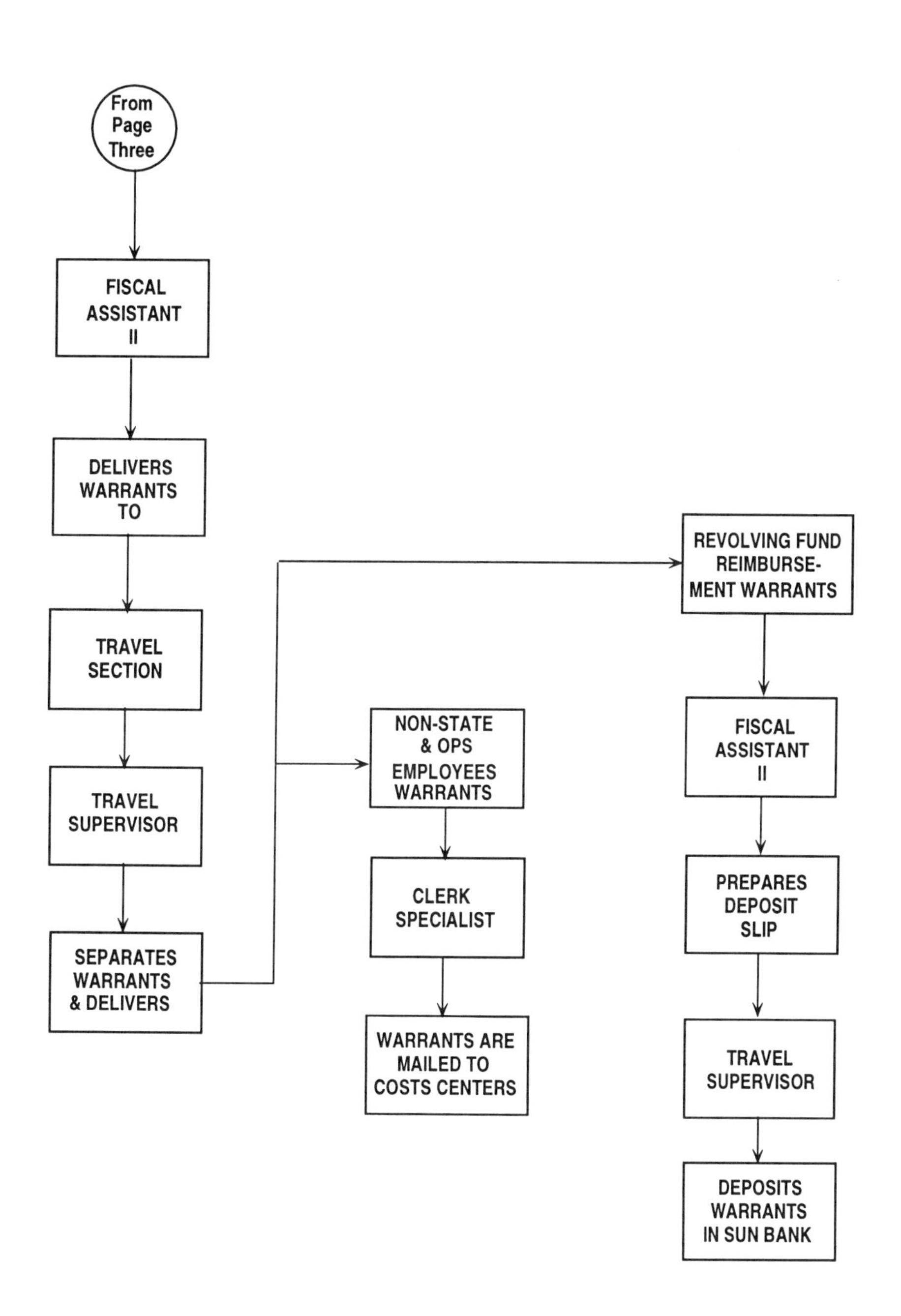
From Page Three
FISCAL ASSISTANT II
DELIVERS WARRANTS TO
TRAVEL SECTION
TRAVEL SUPERVISOR
SEPARATES WARRANTS & DELIVERS
REVOLVING FUND REIMBURSE-MENT WARRANTS
NON-STATE & OPS EMPLOYEES WARRANTS
CLERK SPECIALIST
WARRANTS ARE MAILED TO COSTS CENTERS
FISCAL ASSISTANT II
PREPARES DEPOSIT SLIP
TRAVEL SUPERVISOR
DEPOSITS WARRANTS IN SUN BANK

WORK-FLOW DIAGRAM

Recall that the "work-flow" diagram is another form of flowchart that makes use of a drawing, often crude, of the movements of people, information or materials. It is rarely used in government, but it is still a valuable tool. The example below uses the process for leasing found earlier in different flowchart and tries to show the movements of the documents across offices.

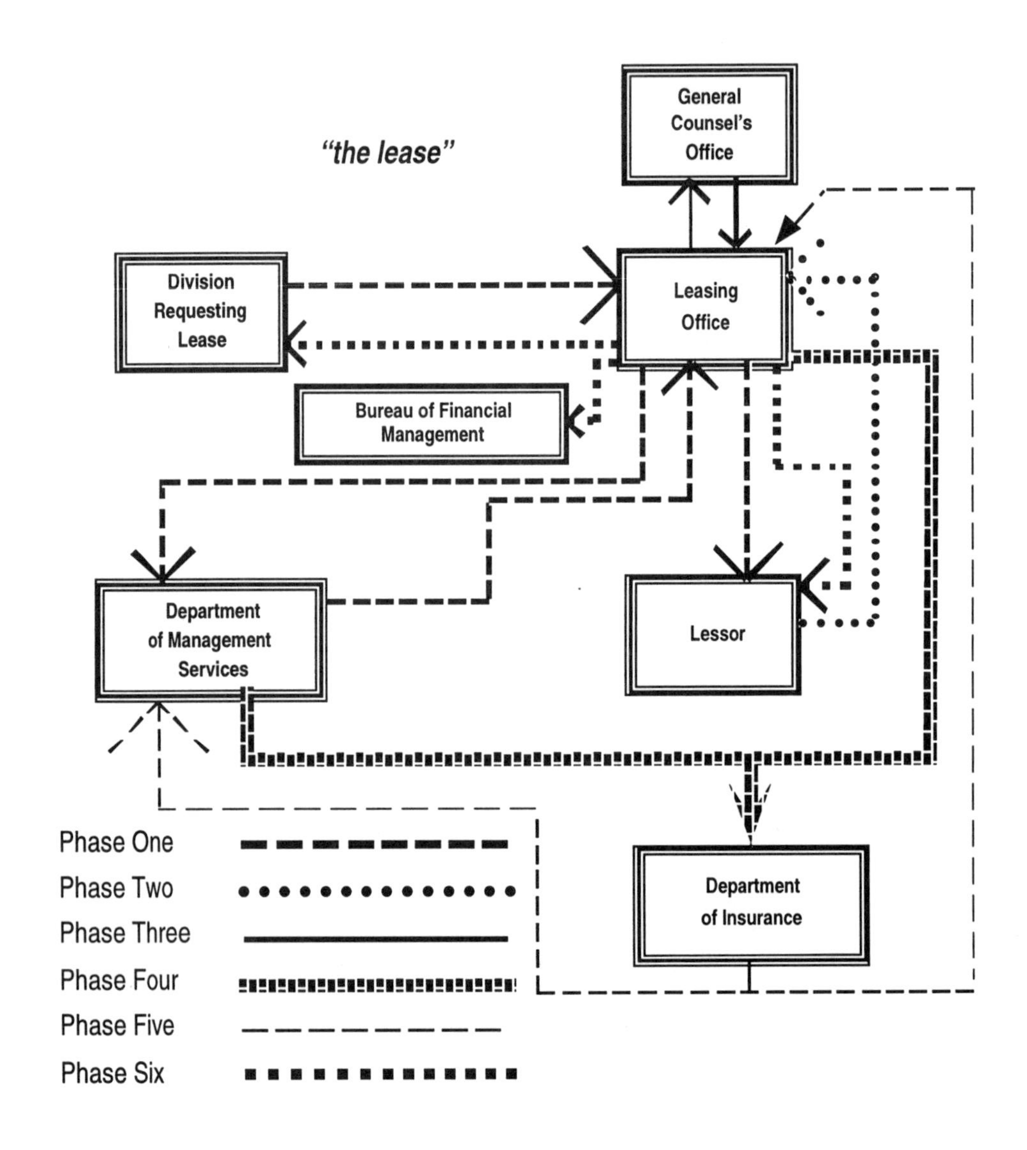

RESPONSIBILITIES WORK CHART

This type of flowchart shows who is going to assume responsibility for each step. We said earlier that this would be a good chart for a family planning a dinner party or a wedding. Shown below is the beginning of a responsibilities work chart by a father who has very little understanding of what is involved in planning a wedding. See if you can improve it. Some people refer to this type of chart as a "deployment chart." Call it what you like.

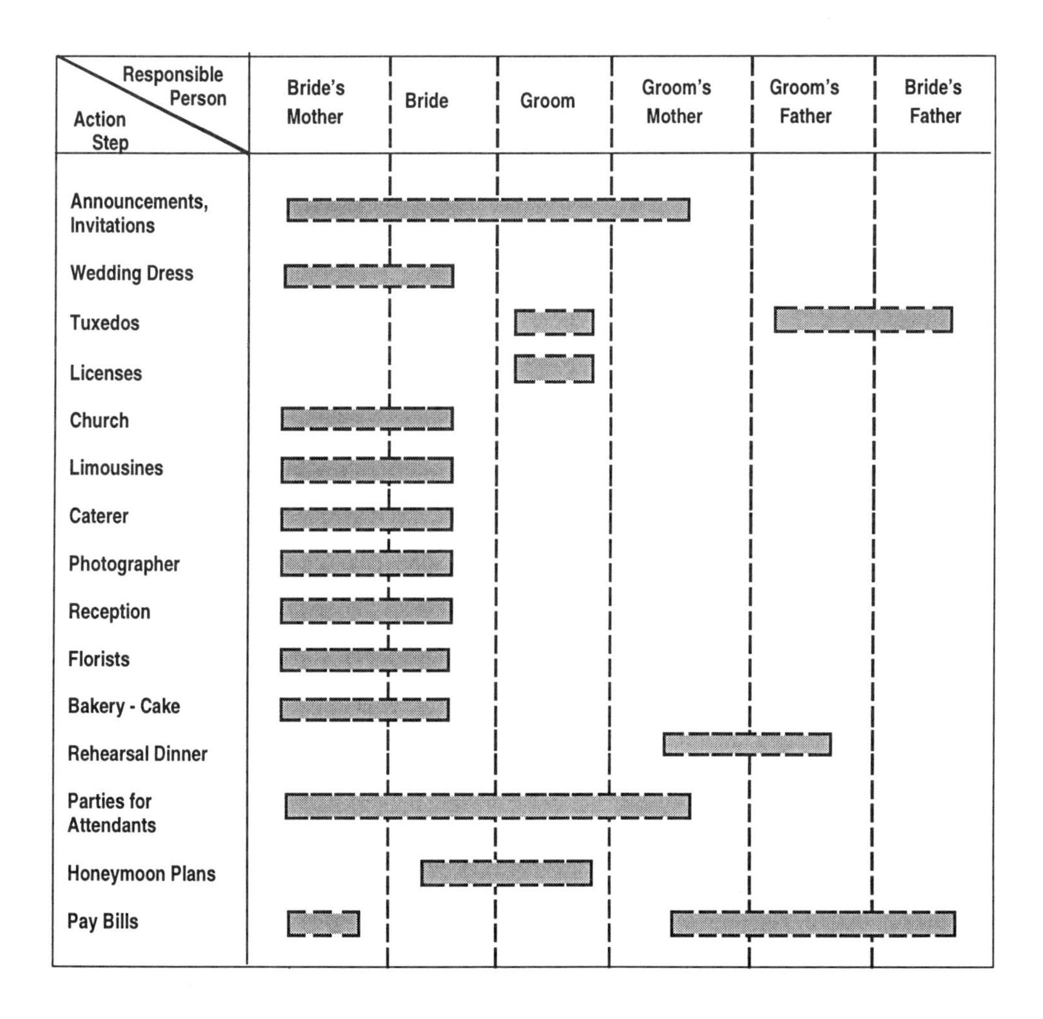

BLUE CHIPS

- The flowchart is such an important tool that we insist that every orientation seminar on quality improvement provide a brief overview of it. The tools seminar that we teach begins with the flowchart. It is basic to an understanding of process. Actually, if new associates were given a copy of flowcharts for the processes they will work in, their in-service training would be enhanced tremendously.
- Care should be taken in defining the limits of the process you are studying and flowcharting. When you are flowcharting, you will undoubtedly list some activities in a rectangle box that represent another sub-process. To indicate this, draw two additional lines in the rectangle to let others know that there is another process contained in this step.
- When first beginning the flowchart, do not try to make it look pretty. You will find that you will be making changes often, and if the chart looks too nice, someone may hesitate to make a correction. This is especially true if one team member spent the better part of a weekend constructing the chart. One technique that we found very useful is to make use of "Post-It Notes." Use them for activity steps and turn them sideways for diamond shapes. "Post" them on a flip chart and feel free to move them about as the team refines the chart. When agreement is reached, you can make the chart more attractive.
- You may wish to place notes on your flowcharts where measurements are taken and where the team thinks that new measurements should be added. Where are customers surveyed on the flowchart? Put stars where a loop might be eliminated. Can the entire process be eliminated?

Question: *If nature used a flowchart, would humans be in a rectangle or a diamond shape symbol?*

10 FORCE FIELD ANALYSIS

WHAT IS IT?

One very helpful technique that teams can use is Force Field Analysis. This technique is described in a variety of ways in the literature, but essentially consists of a method of graphically depicting the "forces" working for and against implementation of a new project or process. It is a way to address the concerns often raised by team members that their deliberations and hard work will likely be in vain because "nothing will ever change."

Force Field Analysis identifies all the various positive and negative forces that will either encourage or discourage change. These forces are graphically displayed and plans can be made to strengthen the positive and eliminate the negative forces. The technique does not simply list the forces, but adds a value to each dependent upon the perceived strength of the factor. For example, a "lack of resources" might receive a weight of "4," vs. "need training," which might be a "2." In other words, the lack of resources is perceived by the team as far more critical to the success of the new idea or project than the lack of trained staff.

WHY DO WE DO IT?

Force Field Analysis can help move a team along in its deliberations because it helps the team identify and recognize the presence of factors that will shape their success. Sometimes team members become discouraged if they think that the process improvement stands little chance for acceptance or implementation. Knowing up front that management resistance may be a factor and how the team will plan to overcome that factor later can help team members concentrate on the task at hand.

WHAT DOES A TEAM NEED TO USE IT?

The facilitator should have a basic understanding of the technique and be equipped with the usual flip chart, markers and masking tape.

HOW DO WE DO IT? WHAT ARE THE RULES?

Step One

The team selects a potential problem that they will work on. This problem may have been identified in a Cause and Effect Diagram, or one found through the study of a Pareto Chart. In any event, the problem is defined, and the definition is placed on the flip chart.

Step Two

The team discusses the various areas that might affect the resolution of the problem. For example, a problem might be "lack of referrals from the community," with potential factors to consider such as "program policy," "visibility in community," etc. The first two steps are shown graphically below.

Problem:
"Lack of Referrals from the Community"
Areas To Study:
Visibility in Community
Program Policy
Resources—Service Funds
Staff

Step Three

Each of the "Areas to Study" is then placed on a separate piece of flip chart paper and considered independently by the team. A line is drawn down the center of the page that is called the "Status Quo" or current condition line. Then, the team facilitator or team leader draws arrows pointing to the center line to indicate the direction of each force. For example:

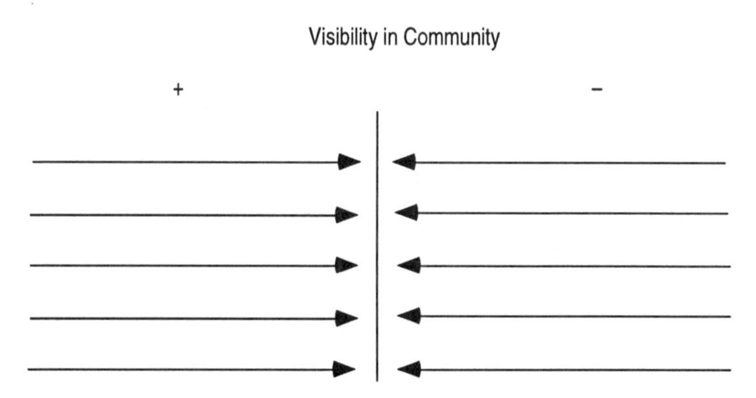

Step Four

The team then discusses the driving (positive and/or supportive), as well as the inhibiting (negative and/or problem) forces at work in the area under consideration. These forces are listed in the appropriate left or right column (+ or –) as shown below.

Step Five

Place a priority on each force by assigning a number indicating its importance. Use a weighted scale from 1–10 with 10 being the highest (most important) rank.

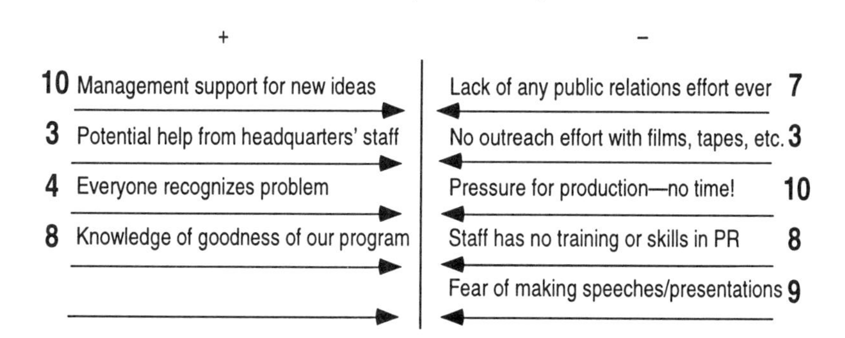

Step Six

The numbers are added up with the totals placed below each column.

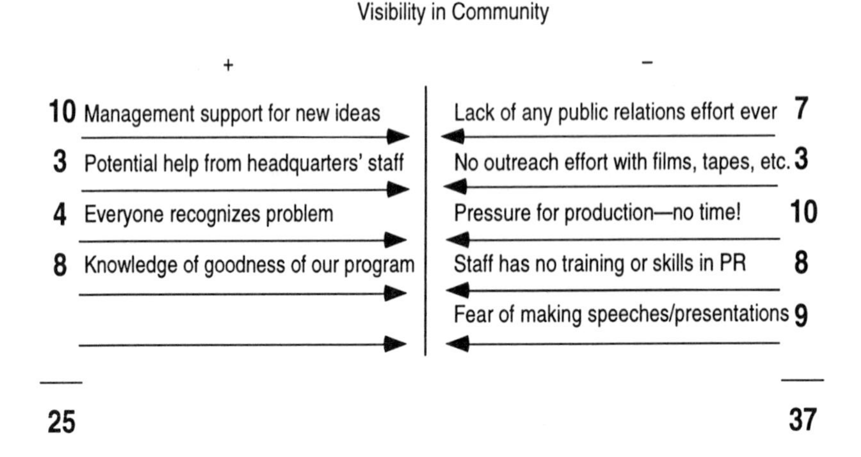

It is now more obvious to the team what forces will help or hinder their efforts. It will also become obvious whether negative or positive forces are stronger, and thus whether the team will have little difficulty improving the process or have their hands full. In our example, the positive forces total 25, while the negative ones total 37. It is clear that, although management support for new ideas is given lip service, little has been done over the years to address this problem. The staff feels a genuine pressure for production (10) and is not that excited about making presentations or speeches.

If the positive forces total higher than the negative, things may improve over time. The reverse is true if the negative outweighs the positive. Things will remain the same or get worse. The difference in the scores indicate a little about how fast conditions are changing— for the good or the bad.

Step Seven

With their analysis complete, the team may select those negative forces that they wish to overcome with the development of a plan. They may also plan how to maximize the positive forces to help them reach their goal. One of the real advantages to the Force Field Analysis is that the team is given the opportunity to see the possibilities for change and positive improvement.

11 HISTOGRAMS

Histograms pose some problems for students in our classes. Just looking at tables of data, "ranges" and "intervals" is overwhelming for some people who believe that they will never understand this tool, and reasons for not using it begin to appear very logical. Why not stick with the easier tools?

Actually, there is nothing mysterious about a histogram. We promise to take the mystery out of this exceptionally useful tool and provide examples. You will be able to construct histograms with very little effort.

WHAT IS IT?

The histogram is a visual representation of a lot of data. The picture shows the variation in data that would be difficult to interpret if all you had was a set of numbers.

Almost everything we measure can have variation. For example, if we were to measure the time it takes for a customer to see an interviewer in a state agency, we would probably see a great deal of variation. Perhaps, if the customer is fortunate, she will be seen in 15 minutes, while another might have to wait 35. The waiting time varies depending upon when the customer arrives at the office.

The histogram helps display this variance in data in a scientific way so that it is easier to see variations, patterns, etc. If a second histogram is developed with data taken at a different office, or perhaps on a different day, comparison of the two histograms might be useful to the team as they address improvements in the process.

A histogram may look like a simple bar chart, but it contains more information. In fact, the creation of the histogram is credited to a French man, A. M. Guerry, who was interested in showing how crime was affected by the age of the criminal. Rather than merely showing the number of crimes in a bar chart, Guerry went one step further and showed how crime was influenced by the age of the criminal through the use of a histogram. His charts clearly showed the number of crimes by age category—something that had not been done before.

In fact, a histogram is a bar chart of a frequency distribution of a continuous variable. Examples of continuous variables include time, length, age, count, etc. The histogram shows the relative frequency of occurrence of the data being examined, displays the distribution of the data, and demonstrates the extent to which the data approximates the expected type of curve. In the following example, the histogram represents "ages" of customers of an agency in government.

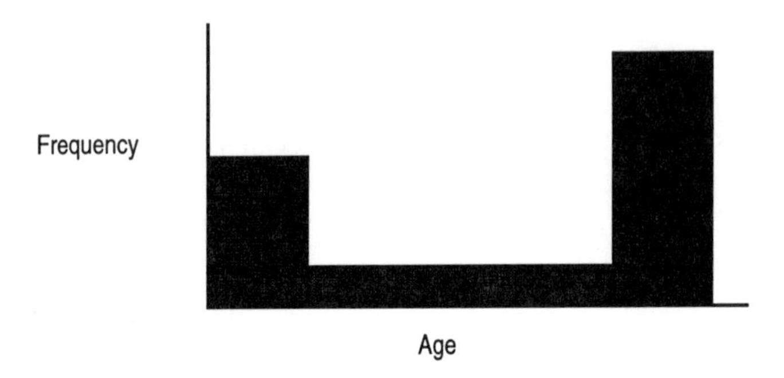

This is not a actual histogram, but represents an unusual display of data. Perhaps it is a Social Security Office where the "customers" are children getting their Social Security cards, and senior citizens applying for benefits. Note the unusual shape of the histogram in this example. We say unusual because it has two "humps," one showing when the children came in for their cards and the other showing when the senior citizens came in. The shape of a histogram can reveal a great deal about the data. The importance of the shape, where the histogram's "center" is, how wide it is, and whether it is "skewed" right or left will be discussed later.

WHY SHOULD IT BE USED?

When a team collects its data, it will become apparent that what they have is a collection of numbers that appear to be interesting, but which can be difficult to interpret. What can we say about the following waiting times observed in an unemployment waiting line?

 # minutes

31	**12**	**41**	**26**	**18**
27	**32**	**22**	**17**	**16**

It is obvious that there is variation. But what else can we say about it? What is the pattern? A histogram can show us. It is a picture of our data.

WHAT DOES A TEAM NEED TO USE IT?

Data and a basic understanding of the steps to construct the histogram are all that the team needs. If the histogram resulting from your data is really unusual, you may wish to share it with managers in your headquarters office or a statistician. Follow the steps outlined below with your own data.

Step One

Collect the data and place it in a table.

51	53	44	48	57	41
55	22	53	63	45	39
34	43	65	59	62	73
43	66	49	61	59	78
44	41	15	33	57	34
71	27	39	49	53	47
46	57	43	67	46	53
35	35	44	35	48	75
46	42	62	49	65	33
42	55	51	48	49	67

Step Two

Count the number of data points. In our example we have six columns with ten numbers in each. Thus we have 60 data points. We use the capital letter "**N**" to designate this number. Thus,

$$N = 60$$

Step Three

Find the range of the data. The range is the difference between the largest number and the smallest number.

	Largest =	**78**
minus the	**Smallest=**	**15**
	Range =	**63**

Step Four

In this step, split the data into "**intervals**" or what some people call "**cells**" that will represent the bars of the histogram. We know that we have 60 data points (***Step Two***) and given this information, we can refer to a standard table of numbers that will help us select the number of intervals (or cells) that we will have for our histogram.

N (or # of data points)	# of Intervals (or Cells)
< 30	**Try a Scatter Diagram**
30–50	**6–8**
50–100	**8–11**
100–250	**11–16**

The number of data points in our example was 60 **(N=60)**, therefore the number of **intervals** or **cells** can be 8, 9, 10, or 11. You can decide. For this example we will pick "**9**" as our interval. It could just as easily be "8," "10" or "11." Just remember that the interval or cell is merely a subdivision of the range.

Step Five

Calculate the cell width. This is done with a simple formula:

Cell Width	=	**Range / # of Intervals (or Cells)**
	=	**63 / 9**
	=	**7**

In our example, we were lucky to have a range of exactly 63 and a "9" for our number of Intervals. This will not always be the case, and you will often need to round off when your answer is a decimal. If the range was 67, for instance, the cell width would be 9.5714. We would then round this off to a more convenient number like "10."

Now that we have our Cell Width, we can list our cell boundaries. We take our lowest number and then make certain that there are a total of 7 numbers in the first interval; thus it will be from **15 through 21.**

15 16 17 18 19 20 21

The second interval will be from **22 through 28.**

Note that the intervals are mutually exclusive. We can not have one interval from 15 through 21 and the next interval from 21 through 27. If we did this, what interval would we use for the number 21? It could fit in two intervals!

All data measurements must fit into one, and only one, interval length.

Step Six

Construct a frequency table. Place the interval # and interval length in a table as follows:

Interval #	Interval Length	Frequency	Total
1	15–21		
2	22–28		
3	29–35		
4	36–42		
5	43–49		
6	50–56		
7	57–63		
8	64–70		
9	71–77		
10	78–84		

To complete the frequency table, we refer to our original data and place each data point in the appropriate row (i.e., the interval length in which it is found).

51	53	44	48	57	41
55	22	53	63	45	39
34	43	65	59	62	73
43	66	49	61	59	78
44	41	15	33	57	34
71	27	39	49	53	47
46	57	43	67	46	53
35	35	44	35	48	75
46	42	62	49	65	33
42	55	51	48	49	67

Interval #	Interval Length	Frequency	Total
1	15–21	X	1
2	22–28	XX	2
3	29–35	XXXXX XX	7
4	36–42	XXXXX X	6
5	43–49	XXXXX XXXXX XXXXX XXX	18
6	50–56	XXXXX XXX	8
7	57–63	XXXXX XXXX	9
8	64–70	XXXXX	5
9	71–77	XXX	3
10	78–84	X	1

Do you see the "hidden" histogram in the previous table?

Try turning the page sideways. Look at the "X's" in the Frequency box. This is a primitive histogram! We can now construct an actual histogram using the data above.

Step Seven

Refer to the drawing at the top of the next page. First draw the vertical axis to represent the # of times a data point appears in each interval. The largest number is **18**, so "20" will be at the top of the line. Number all the way down to **0** at the bottom. Then draw a horizontal line and label each of the ten intervals in accordance with the Interval Lengths in the table (i.e., **15–21, 22–28, 29–35,** etc.). Using the data in the Frequency box above, fill in a bar at each interval representing frequency of waiting times.

Step Eight

The histogram is now complete but warrants a closer look. We can tell a lot from just looking at this creation. No longer do we just have a maze of numbers without any pattern. What does the "picture" show?

1. It appears to be what is generally called a "normal" distribution. The data appears to generate what we frequently find in nature—a "bell-shape" curve. A lot of the data is in the center with few data points at each end. There are two little "valleys" at the 36-42 and 50-56 intervals, but this is nothing unusual. There are no real surprises. The people waiting in this unemployment line can expect to be "in and out" of the office in from 29 to 63 minutes with a little luck. In fact, 48 out of 60 people did this in our sample (80%).

2. The histogram is not lopsided. Statisticians would say that the distribution is symmetrical, with almost an equal number of measurements above and below the average.

3. There is a fair amount of variability. The shortest time is 15 minutes and the longest is 78 minutes. With less variability we would find a low number of perhaps 34, and a high of 56 minutes. One might ask why it takes one customer

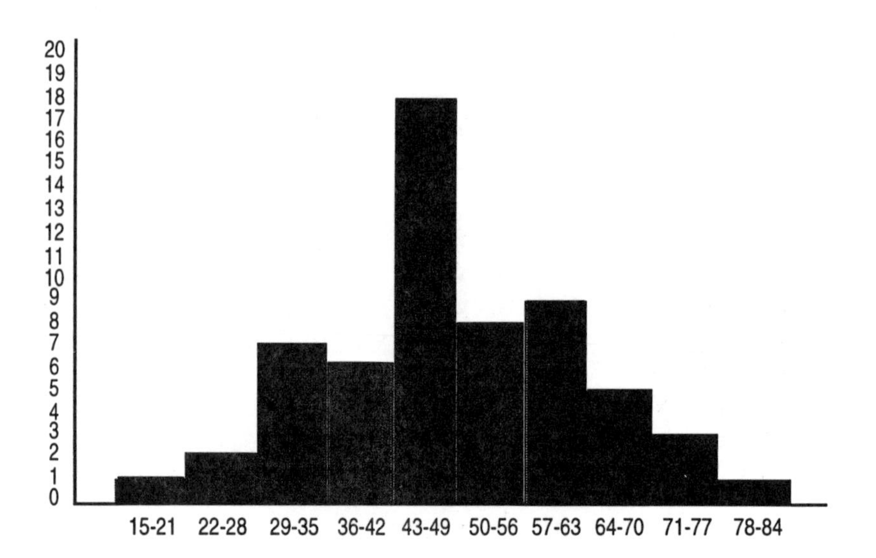

78 minutes while another customer was in and out in 15. What is happening in this process that causes so much variability?

4. There is only one peak—18 data points fall in the 43-49 interval. This confirms that chances are only one process is under study. If there are two peaks, chances are good that two processes are at work. In our example, twin peaks might reveal one group of customers getting served completing all paperwork, and thus taking longer, while another group of customers departs quickly to go home for information they need to process their application.

5. Perhaps we gathered the wrong data. That is OK. We can always go back and do it again. For example, we measured the number of minutes each customer was in the office. The time included initial discussion with a "greeter" who asked the customer to wait until the interviewer was ready, waiting time, interview time, and time for completion of paperwork. Customers differ in the information they bring with them. Types of applications differ (in-state, out-of-state, etc.), and some applications take longer. Good service requires individual attention.

But no one likes to wait. A better measure of customer service might be to measure actual waiting time to see how long each customer actually sits just waiting.

On the following pages are several different histograms showing a wide range of variation and patterns. Interpretations are provided so that you may see how valuable histograms are in facilitating continual improvement.

Examples of different patterns provided by histograms

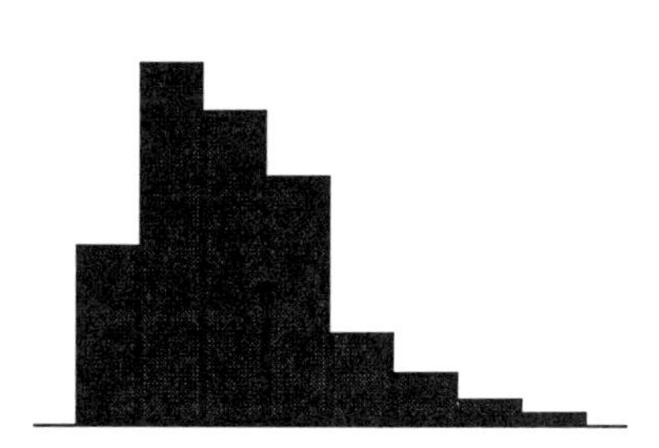

Time of Arrival During Day

This histogram was developed to see when customers arrived during the day at a state jobs office. Note that most arrived during the morning hours (the first four bars, representing 8:30–9:30, 9:31–10:30; 10:31–11:30, and 11:31–12:30). The afternoons were very light. This histogram represents one that is **skewed**. It is *skewed to the left* because the data points fall to the left of what might be considered center. The team studying this histogram might consider what improvements could be made to "even out" the flow of customers or to change work schedules to meet the demands in the morning.

When Marketing Representatives Call Upon Employers

This is a histogram that shows which days of the week marketing representatives have appointments to visit employers to develop jobs. It is readily apparent that Tuesdays and Thursdays are the favorites. A histogram with "twin" peaks often suggests that two processes are under study in the sample. In this case marketing representatives may actually be helping out on Mondays when the offices are busy, and completing paperwork back in the office on Wednesdays and Fridays.

This "**plateau**" histogram does not tell us very much. There is no peak, it is not skewed either way and therefore doesn't help the team very much. The work flow is apparently spread out over the period of time studied, and one might be tempted to say that there are no problems. Something very important may be missing. The data may not be sound. Perhaps the wrong things are being measured. Verify with another tool.

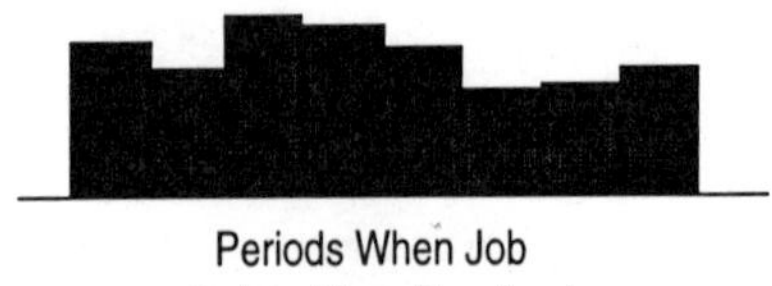

Periods When Job Orders Were Received

A histogram may occasionally have a little data isolated out on its own. In this example, the team was studying the vocational rehabilitation process and how long customers were involved before rehabilitation. They found one who appeared to exceed all expectations. It turns out that this individual was enrolled in a college program that accounted for the extra time. We call this isolated bar of data an "**orphan.**" It does not occur very often, and suggests some *abnormality* that the team may wish to investigate.

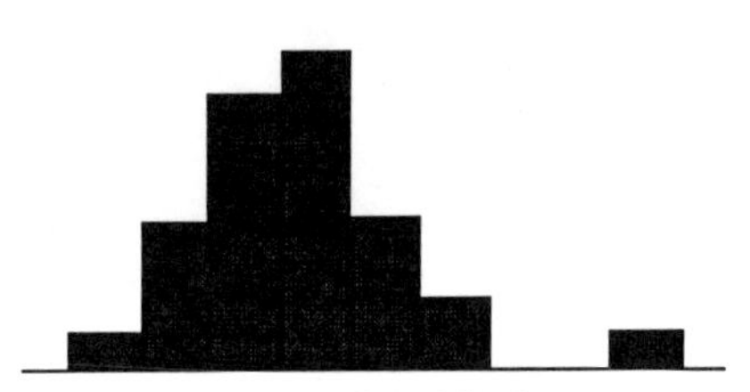

Months to Rehabilitation

This last example of a histogram shows the distribution of a sample of public employees who are "Ecstatic at Work" on any given day. Note that the majority are. Some are happier than others (those to the right of center), while others are not so happy (those to the left of center). Actually this is an example of the classic *bell-shape distribution.* It is rarely, if ever, encountered.

Associates Who Are Ecstatic at Work

BLUE CHIPS

There is a lot more to be learned about histograms. Refer to the wealth of information available at your local or college library. The following points may also help as you study your data.

- You can develop acceptable limits or standards of performance based upon a study of your histogram. You may wish to reduce the variability if your histogram looks like this:
- Be careful when you are collecting data. Make certain that the data represents the way things are right now. Guard against using old data just because it is available. It is better to take the time to collect current numbers.
- Watch the size of your sample. If you reach a conclusion based upon too small a sample, you may be off target. Generally, the bigger the sample, the better. Check back to the table provided in ***Step Four*** to see when you should use a scatter diagram instead of a histogram.
- Remember that the interpretation of your data is the most important consideration. Do not place all your faith in your numbers. They can serve as a guide, but just as important are the other tools at your disposal, like the flowchart and cause and effect diagram.

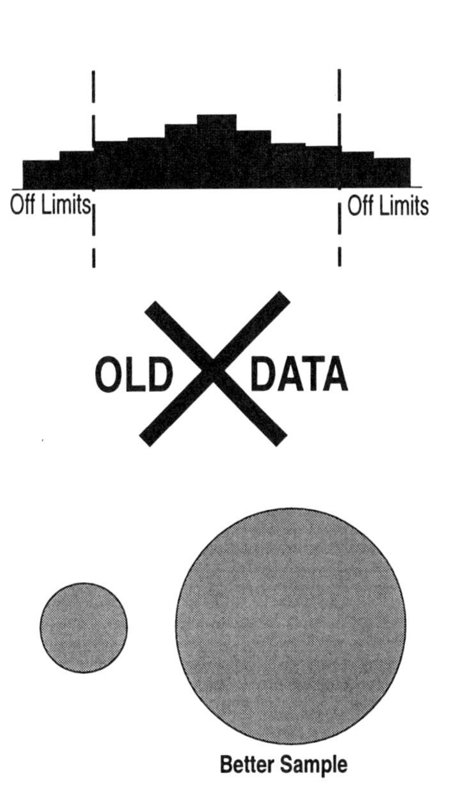

THINK!

12 INTRODUCING CHANGE

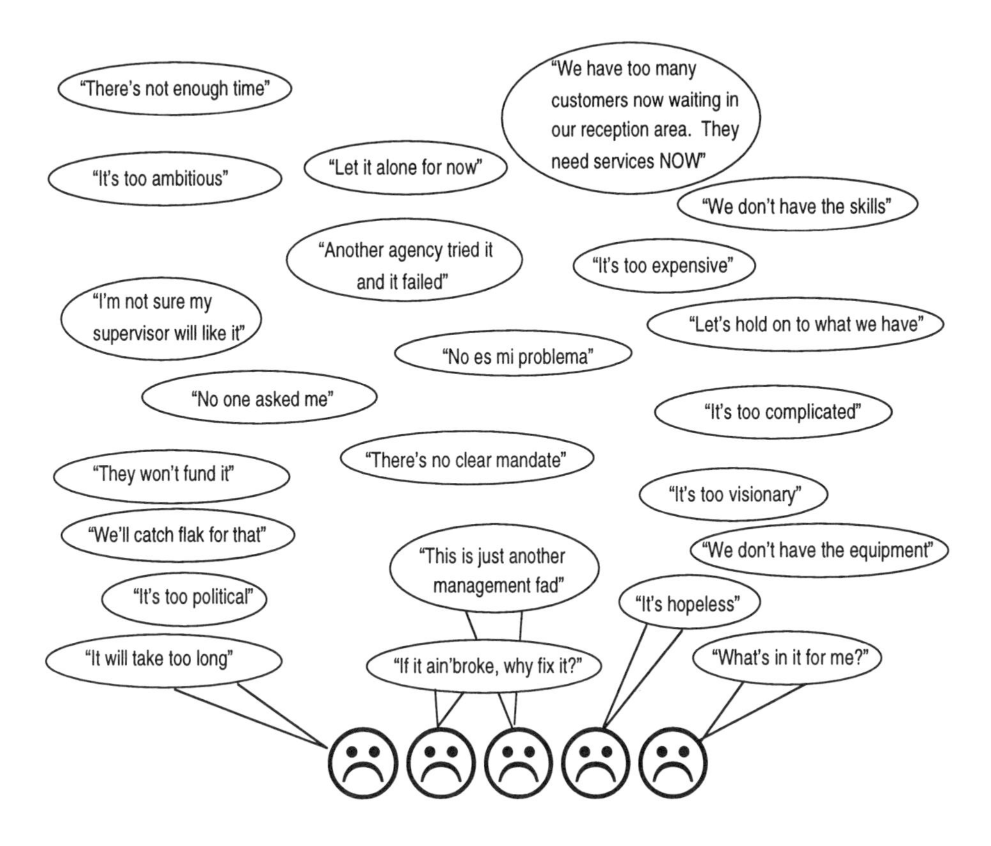

One might question why there is a section on introducing change in a book devoted to continual improvement tools and techniques. We have done this for one simple reason. Every office and team that we have worked with in government faces resistance when the topic of continual improvement or "total quality management" is introduced. The statements above are represent just a few of the reactions we have heard. One of the authors was actually told to leave one office by a supervisor who said, "You will be wasting your time here. We are already a quality office, with quality people. We do not believe in TQM, and do not have time to play around. Take this message back to Tallahassee—stay out!" Although this was an extreme reaction to our offer to assist, it, nevertheless, was not that unusual.

There are many reasons why people resist change. Whenever someone is threatened by another person coming along to interfere with their work, their practices, traditions, status symbols, office location, or beliefs, there is trouble. It is not unusual to find middle management less than supportive of a program that "empowers" their workers. These managers have invested a great deal of time and effort to get in the position they hold. Why would they support a program that empowers front-line workers who may have just joined the agency? If the workers have the power to change the process, determine outcomes and revise policies, what tasks will be left to the supervisor? Is the supervisor that necessary?

Front-line workers are also often resistant to change. They joined a specific agency, and perhaps agreed to an unwritten contract that defined their role and the culture in which they would work. Changes in the process may change this culture, and not give them the satisfaction or benefits to which they have become accustomed. Worse, the process changes may eliminate the need for their position. As a result of their empowerment, they may be out of a job!

During a six-month period, we conducted an informal assessment of where we thought the people in a training program "were" in their acceptance of the potential changes generated by Total Quality Management. Although far from being scientific, we all agreed that the following "histogram" represented acceptance for most of the sessions.

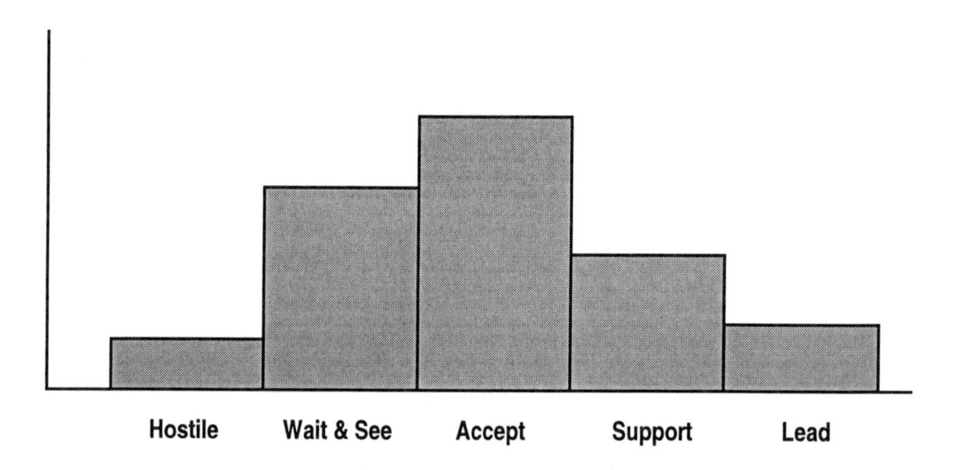

- **Hostile**—This smallest group was openly hostile to the concept of continual improvement. Many in this group were "old-timers" who had "seen it all before." A few were burn-outs who were counting the days to their retirement. Younger associates may have been more hostile internally, but knew enough to give "lip-service" to new proposals by top management.

- **Wait & See**—This large group was composed of people who were sitting on the fence. They were skeptical that Total Quality Management was anything more than the most recent fad. Over the years they had witnessed "Management by Objectives," "Strategic Planning," "Zero-based Budgeting," and "Tactical Planning Management" all come and go. Before committing, they would let a few others jump in and do the initial work.

- **Accept**—The people in this group were ready to accept and commit, but they asked for additional training before joining a team. They also used the excuse that there was little time for teams, that the customers were sitting in the waiting area demanding services, and that the agency should grant monetary rewards if more work after hours and on weekends was necessary. They smiled a lot, but it was obvious they could be lost if they were not nurtured.
- **Support**—To this group, it was obvious that the right formula was being advanced by management. How could anyone argue with customer satisfaction and with having everyone involved on teams to improve the process by making small changes? They immediately joined teams, attended advanced training programs, and stayed after class to discuss the subject with instructors.
- **Lead**—These individuals became disciples. They wanted to become process improvement guides, internal consultants and teachers. We found them enrolled in TQM classes and seminars at the local university. They became active in professional associations focusing on quality, and their lives became consumed with converting others.

A STRATEGY FOR CHANGE

The strategy we developed may not work for your bureau, division or department. We found that it did help us develop changes in our program, and contributed to a gradual acceptance and support for continual improvements. We began with the following Ground Rules and proceeded to poke holes in the circle of resistance with its associated skepticism, cynicism and hostility to change.

OUR GROUND RULES FOR CHANGE

1. **Forget for the moment the Hostile.** When we are successful, they will either join us, leave us or die off. We will waste no resources on them.
2. **Nurture the Leaders.** New recruits to this group will come from the Supporters directly to their left on the histogram. Both leaders and supporters will need additional training, mentoring and new experiences. We will provide special workshops for them, will take them on field trips to places where quality is stressed, and will ask them to become process improvement guides and internal consultants.
3. **Concentrate fully on Accepters.** They will soon move into the Supporter ranks, along with the Wait & See associates. Encourage the formation of teams. Develop training in every office location so that teams will be prepared.

Poking Holes in the Circle of Resistance

Role play with resistors. Reverse positions. Try to come up with reasons why it is not a good idea to serve customers better. What is it about the status quo that is so great? List the reasons why what the organization does is perfect. List the better management methods that should be tried instead of process improvement initiatives.

Treat people nicely and with respect even if they are not supporters. They are not the enemy. Faulty processes in need of improvement are the enemy.

Recognize and identify the leaders in the informal network. These are not the formal leaders (i.e., bureau chiefs, etc.), but rather those people awarded this status by the "worker bees" who get the job done. Every organization has them. They can make or break any new initiative. Success is assured with their support; without it, failure is more likely. Help them embrace the need for change and the value of customer focus.

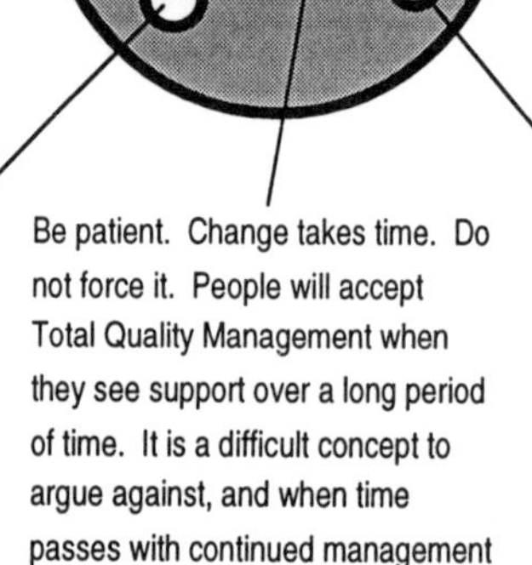

When you begin, start small. Do a pilot and test before going organization-wide. Risk is reduced, costs are small, and the hostile ignore the process.

Celebrate every success, regardless of size. Every improvement is important. Reward teams with recognition in newsletters. Present certificates and plaques. Notify their home newspapers. Have "Quality Celebration Days—The Best of the Best" and invite the Governor to attend. Take your Quality Council into the field and celebrate locally at every opportunity.

Be patient. Change takes time. Do not force it. People will accept Total Quality Management when they see support over a long period of time. It is a difficult concept to argue against, and when time passes with continued management support, the change will occur.

Involve everyone when you begin. Lack of involvement leads to resentment, which generates resistance.
Concentrate on the"Wait & See" group.

BLUE CHIPS

The introduction of continual improvement is actually a **small** change. What associates are asked to do is to improve existing processes through small changes to increase customer satisfaction. This is not the same kind of change organizations to through with wholesale reorganizations, reengineering, layoffs, and retrenchments.
Let us compare the traditional approach to change where major innovations have been the key to success to the approach taken by the Japanese where they prefer gradual, unending improvements, doing "little things" better. They call this the "Kaizen" key to success. With which approach would you feel the "most" changes?

	Kaizen *	**Innovation**
Effect	Long-term and long-lasting but undramatic	Short-term, but dramatic
Pace	Small steps	Big steps
Time frame	Continuous and incremental	Intermittent/non-incremental
Change	Gradual and constant	Abrupt and volatile
Involvement	Everybody	Select few
Approach	Collectivism, group efforts, systems approach	Rugged individualism, individual ideas and efforts
Mode	Maintenance and improvement	Scrap and rebuild
Spark	Conventional know-how and state of the art	Technological breakthroughs, new inventions, new theories
Practical requirements	Requires little investment, but great effort to maintain	Requires large investment, but little effort to maintain
Effort orientation	People	Technology
Evaluation criteria	Process and efforts for better results	Results for profits

* Taken from Kaizen, The Key to Japan's Competitive Success by Masaaki Imai

13 MAKING PRESENTATIONS

THE FEARS WE FACE

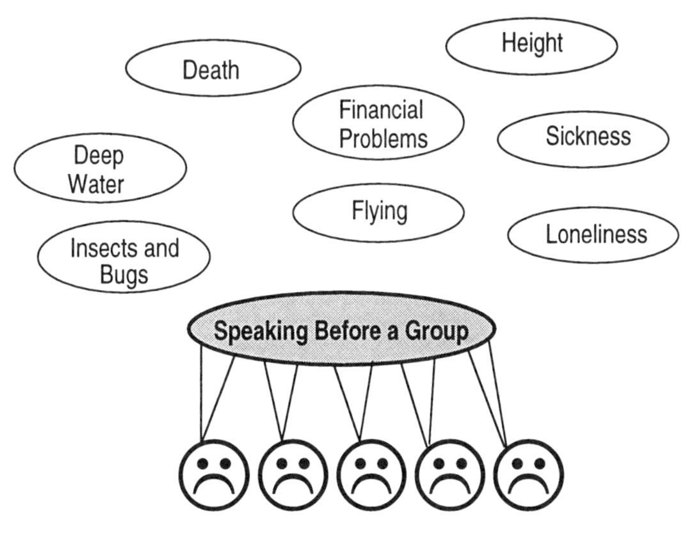

R. H. Bruskin Associates has conducted surveys over the years asking people what they fear most. Is it flying, height, financial problems, or even death itself? No. What we fear more than all else is: ***Speaking before a Group***

So what do we do to our most valued staff? What do we ask of those who have toiled many hours to define and develop process improvements? How do we reward them for their devotion to increased customer satisfaction? How do we thank them for this effort?

We ask them to stand up in front of a panel, sometimes called a "Quality Council," to make a presentation. Often, this council is composed of top management—the secretary of their department, the division directors, bureau chiefs, and worst of all, some of their own peers.

What a system!

These authors have on more than one occasion been told that the management presentation is the most hated and feared part of Total Quality Management. However, *there is a way to resolve this fear.*

Many of the ideas presented here were taken from an outstanding book, *I Can See You Naked—A Fearless Guide to Making Great Presentations* by Ron Hoff. Ron has made hundreds of presentations over his lifetime and has taught thousands the skills of making outstanding presentations. The book, first published in 1988, is the *premier guide* and best written text on this important subject. The research mentioned earlier by R. H. Bruskin is discussed in this book.

WHAT IS IT?

The **management presentation** is an opportunity for teams to show how a process can be improved or how a problem can be resolved.

WHY SHOULD IT BE USED?

The best reason it may be useful is because management in your agency requires a presentation. Once the team really understands the steps they can take to overcome their fears, they too will appreciate the opportunity to present. The team should feel honored. How often in one's career does the chance to meet with top management occur? It is a rare opportunity. In this instance the Quality Council has determined that a team has something important to say. Furthermore, they want to hear it in person. You and your team know more about the subject than they do. The team has spent considerable time examining a specific process, collected data, flowcharted, studied potential solutions, tried a few out, and finally come prepared to recommend an improvement. Not one person on the council is as aware of what is happening as any member of the team.

WHEN DO WE USE IT?

The management presentation is generally done at the end of the problem identification and solution process. At this point the team is ready to present their findings to the council for consideration, approval and implementation. Often the team may be called upon to make several presentations. These may include one at their regional office level, one at the division headquarters, and a final one to the department's council. The first two presentations are somewhat like a dress rehearsal for the grand presentation. Any rough spots can be ironed out during the early presentations.

HOW DO WE DO IT? WHAT ARE THE RULES?

There are no rules. There are, however, guidelines for good presentations that have been developed over the years. Ron Hoff, in his book mentioned earlier, has hundreds of suggestions in over 250 pages. Many more are found in other books on making speeches and presentations. We believe the following guidelines taken from our seminar on making presentations offer a good beginning.

GUIDELINES FOR SUCCESSFUL MANAGEMENT PRESENTATIONS

1. **People want you to succeed.** Members of the Quality Council (or whatever your agency calls the management group to which presentation are made) are people who *want you to succeed.* They have an investment in the success of the quality program. They must count on teams like yours for success. They do not want you to fail. They will in all likelihood not ask difficult questions because

   a. They do not want to embarrass you with a tough question that you have difficulty answering.

   b. They do not want to embarrass themselves, for they know full well that the team knows more about the process than they do.

   c. If they get the reputation of giving teams a hard time, there will be fewer teams who will ever become ready enough to present. Teams will not take the chance on being given a bad time if the council is perceived as hard-nosed.

2. **Council members are human.** They dress the same way as everyone else. They also fear making presentations and will do their best to help the team succeed. They are definitely "on your side."

3. **Do not *ever* read your presentation.** The worst thing that a team can do is put one of their members up in front of the council with a "prepared" address. Use limited **key words** on a three-by-five card which can be referred to periodically. Pretend that you're telling a story to a group of your friends. You will already know a great deal about what your team did. In the following example, note that the **key words** *remind* you what you're planning to cover, keep track of your progress and do not require constant attention.

   The following set of "presentation cards" is an example of what might work for a team. It is acceptable to read things like the mission statement and goals, which tend to be very specific. The next two cards provide **key words** only.

#1

Name of Our Team: "Stuart Aviators"

Team Members: Donna Bognar, Ruth Gribbin-Schmitt, Pamela Devercelly, Sylvia Boucher

Mission Statement: The mission of the Unemployment Claims Office is to: Alleviate hardships associated with unemployment by providing prompt and accurate benefits for eligible workers who become unemployed through no fault of their own.

#2

Values:
Respect for one another
Every team member's contribution is equally important
Sense of pride in accomplishments
Maintain sense of humor
Sharing recognition

#3

What We Did...

- **Saw long waiting lines**
- **Customer complaints**
- **Surveyed customers**
- **Flow charted**
- **Bar Graphs**
- **Brainstormed**

#4

What We Did...

- **Proposal for pilot**
- **Office of Communication - press**
- **Tracked for baseline**
- **Changes in process**
- **Results**
- **Any questions?**

These four cards provide a framework for a 15–20 minute presentation. Actually the four cards could easily be placed on an overhead transparency to project on a screen. Then the presenter would not even have to handle any three-by-five cards. On the other hand, the team may wish to reserve the overhead for transparencies showing data studied, flow charts, etc.

4. **Celebrate your nervousness.** This is a sign that you really care about doing a good job. If you did not care, you would not "feel those butterflies" in your stomach. Everyone who wants to do a good job is nervous. No good actor, comedian or officer in an association ever appears before as group without feeling nervous. They *all* have butterflies. They *all* feel some degree of fear. It is said that some very famous persons have actually gotten physically ill prior to a speech, presentation or appearance on stage.

   Nervousness is *actually very good*, if we know how to use it to our advantage. "When you have butterflies in your stomach, get them to fly in formation..."

   Stress can be somewhat helpful during presentations, if you recognize it and use it to your advantage. Here are some tips to channel those butterflies:

   a. Recognize the stress and learn to love it. It is an ally and a signal that something great is about to happen. There is little chance that life will be boring for the next few minutes. Know that this good feeling (the stress, the butterflies) will probably pass in a few minutes, once you are into your presentation. You will be on your own without your friend. But do not worry, he will be back the next time you get ready to present. He will *never* leave you forever, because he is your true friend.

   b. *Never* tell the council or any audience about your nerves. Just don't mention your discomfort.

   c. Play a mental and physical game just before you go on. If possible, take a brisk walk to "charge-up." Walking will loosen you up and will burn off a little energy. Your knees will be in better shape and less likely to shake. Tell yourself that you are the luckiest person in the world at that moment. You get to have people actually listen to you with their full attention. You will not have the usual interruptions in normal conversation. The stage is yours. The very best speakers all "warm up" with similar techniques. They get their juices flowing!

d. If you find that you cannot get up to take a walk, do something. Actually it is rare that you will not have a few moments to walk before your presentation. There are usually breaks between team presentations. However, if you find yourself sitting for thirty minutes just prior to your presentation, do the following:

- Do not sit with your legs crossed. It might just be your luck that one of them will "fall asleep," and you will have difficulty walking when you are called. Wiggle your toes and gently twirl your wrists a little to keep the circulation going. Let your arms drop naturally
- Check your jaw. Does it feel tense? Loosen it up a bit by wiggling it gently.
- Take a few deep breaths.
- Put a smile on your face, *act* as if there is no other place on the planet that you would rather be, and your audience will be with you.

5. **Give yourself a pep talk**. Just before you go on, take a few minutes to think positive thoughts. This is a trick that almost all good speakers know. They sometimes do it in their dressing room, or while they are physically "charging up" (see step 3). The script they use may differ from speaker to speaker, but it can go something like this:

   "What a great day for me. Here I am getting ready to tell these people what our team has been doing for the past six months. There is not one person on the council that knows as much as I do about this improvement. I've studied it more than they have, flowcharted it, and know the steps our team went through to get where we are. This council is ready to hear what we have done. They want to see that they were very wise by empowering us to come up with these ideas. They are good people who want me to do well."

6. **Do not worry about your hands**. Do not fold them across your chest. It may look defensive. Do not be concerned about where to put them. A little trick that some speakers use is to merely let them hang naturally at your side. If you feel like you must hold on to something "to be in touch with your self," just touch your thumb to your forefinger on each hand. No one will notice this little touch, but you will know that you are still alive and warm. Far better to do this than to grasp your hands together, place a strangle hold on the podium, clutch chalk or a pointer, or play with a pencil. Believe us, we have seen speakers do all of this and more.

7. **Change position**. If you stand still for long in one place, the audience may think that you have died with your feet planted on the floor. Look at the popular speakers. They all move around. Talk show hosts even walk into the audience. The audience never knows where he will show up. You need not walk into the council's area, but merely from side to side a bit. It will help reduce tension and will keep the audience more alert.

8. **Show your enthusiasm and intensity.** Who else in the room should be more enthusiastic or intense about your team's recommendations than you? You will never get the council to be excited about your team's work unless you are. We have seen more than one presenter succeed merely because of their enthusiasm. An enthusiastic presentation is infectious. When a presenter is "into" the subject, there is a magic in the room that infects others. The opposite is also true. The team's idea may be an outstanding one, but if delivered in a boring manner, it will not get the attention it deserves.

   Enthusiasm can be faked. That is, it can be as long as you truly believe in the recommendations proposed. The enthusiasm must have a firm foundation of fact upon which it is built. People rarely question a person's enthusiasm for a good idea, especially when they realize the amount of work a team completed to arrive at the recommendation. In many ways, the presenter is a salesperson. When have you seen a new car salesperson who was not enthusiastic about his or her product? The successful salesperson truly believes in the product and is enthusiastic.

9. **KISS.** In other words, **K**eep **I**t **S**hort, **S**tupid. Even though you may be having a grand time, and the council is really giving you good feedback, respect the time allotted. When things are going well, it is too easy to overextend your presentation. Audiences' attention spans are short, regardless of their support, especially if there are multiple presentations. You may ask another member of your team to stand in the back of the room to signal when to stop.

10. **Use overheads that the council can read**. If you are going to use an overhead projector, be certain that your overhead transparencies have *minimal* information per sheet. Do not copy an entire page of typewritten narrative or a table of data that cannot easily be read from the back of the room. Such a transparency is an insult to the council and the rest of your audience. Better to place three or four words or statistics per transparency, and use more transparencies.

11. **Practice using the overhead**. Note now the transparency should be placed on the projector so that you are not flipping it over or turning it around needlessly. Believe it or not, there is just one way that is right. When you get it right during practice, place a small mark or number in the upper right hand corner. Then, always place the transparency on the projector with the symbol in the upper right hand corner.

    Better yet. Get another member of your team to be in charge of placing the transparencies. That way you can give your full attention to the presentation and the council's feedback.

12. **Get Feedback**. Knowing how the council is perceiving your remarks is critical. How do you do this? Watch their eyes. Their eyes will tell whether they are following along, whether they are questioning your remarks, or whether they are lost.

DESIGNING EFFECTIVE OVERHEADS

There are complete books devoted to good graphics presentations. The suggestions below are from an article by Sue Hinkin in the January, 1995 issue of *Presentations.*

- **Use Upper and Lower Case for Body Text.** It is critical that the Quality Council be able to read the text as quickly and effortlessly as possible. Here is an example

  Use upper and lower case for body text.

  Use UPPER CASE only to call attention and for major headings or titles.

- **Use large type for Easy Reading**
- **Choose simple typefaces.** If you are using a computer, choose Helvetica, Arial, Geneva or Avante Garde typefaces.
- **Choose sans serif typefaces.** These are the ones without little attachments, and thus appear clean and crisp.
- **Highlight important ideas with bold print and italics**. The council should not have to try to figure out what is important. Bold print calls the most attention, then italics. A little goes a long way. Do not overuse either **bold** or *italic*.
- **Be consistent**. Text size, style, spacing and positioning should be consistent. If you are lucky enough to have presentation software on your computer, use it and choose one style.
- **Keep it simple**. Simplicity is the essence of an effective presentation.

To summarize, which example below would look best on an overhead? Why?

The *best* way to demonstrate importance to an audience would be to use **bold** typefaces whenever **you want** to emphasize a part of your overall *presentation* in front of that audience regardless of where you are.	**Bold = Attention**

13. **Save handouts to the end**. If you pass out any material prior to the end of your presentation, you will lose part of your audience. They will be reading. Then you will not be able to see their eyes, will not get any feedback and will not be certain they heard you. They cannot read and listen at the same time.

14. **Know your Council**. Chances are you will already know who is on the council, but if you do not, find out their names, titles and divisions of the agency they represent. If you demonstrate that you know them and their names, they may remember yours.

15. **Watch your humor**. Humor is a dangerous thing if directed at anyone except yourself. Be careful not be "cute" with remarks about where the council members work. Their work may be the butt of jokes within the organization, but they may take their jobs seriously. Personal remarks are inappropriate.

16. **Be prepared for the unexpected.** We live in an imperfect world. For example, just as you are three transparencies into your presentation, the bulb on the overhead burns out. What do you do? First of all, things you **should not** do are: (a) blame the person who gave you the projector or the person running it; (b) get mad; or (c) just stand there.

    Instead, admit that this is an imperfect world and that a new bulb will be located. Ask if there are any questions thus far. Wing it and go on with the presentation by summarizing the overheads on a flip chart. Take a short break while a new bulb is located. "Chill out"—this is not the end of the world.

17. **Anticipate questions.** Learn to love questions. They show the fact that the council has listened to your presentation and thought enough of it to pay attention. There are several ways to prepare for these questions.

    a. Anticipate what questions you may be asked. Have team members "brainstorm" with possible questions the council members might ask. Then develop answers and rehearse them. Someone may ask how the improvement will help customers. Another may ask about how the team surveyed the customers.

    b. If you cannot answer a question, admit it. You may turn to another team member for a response. If no one has the answer, write down the question while you are standing before the council and offer to get an answer within a specified period of time (three days, etc.).

18. **Be prepared**. Make sure you thoroughly know your team, the mission, values, and the process studied. Know who your customers are and how they were surveyed. Have at least seven times more information than you will share with the council. **Rehearse** your presentation exactly as you will make it. Use your overheads. Talk to the council rather than to the screen.

19. **Always seek to improve**. You can always improve your presentations. When you are finished, write down what you think went well and what needs improvement. Look forward to your next opportunity to present. Consult Hoff's book and get constructive criticism from team members.

14 MILESTONE CHARTS

There is one simple tool that can be very helpful to a team. It is the "Milestone Chart."

WHAT IS IT?

A **Milestone Chart** is a graphic representation of the team's progress.

WHY SHOULD IT BE USED?

The Milestone Chart helps a team see its progress toward their goal. Without one, it may become difficult to see progress. The chart can also help keep assignments organized, and in many ways resembles the "responsibilities work chart" discussed earlier under flowcharting (see Example 1 next page).

WHAT DOES A TEAM NEED TO USE IT?

The only requirement is a blank sheet of poster paper, a ruler and a marker.

HOW DO WE USE IT? WHAT ARE THE RULES?

1. List all the required actions in chronological order on the "Y" axis.
2. Enter consecutive week ending dates across the "X" axis.
3. Draw a line for each step between the start and completion dates.
4. Place the name of the responsible person or group beside each action.

In addition to the milestone chart, there is one additional variant of this tool that might even be more helpful to the team. If added to the list of activities, responsible persons and due date, this chart can track who else should be involved at each step, the budget assigned, space to keep interested persons informed of your progress (like your supervisors or directors), potential roadblocks, etc. You are free to decide exactly what kinds of items you wish to track and have data on at any given step in the process (see Example 2 next page).

EXAMPLE 1

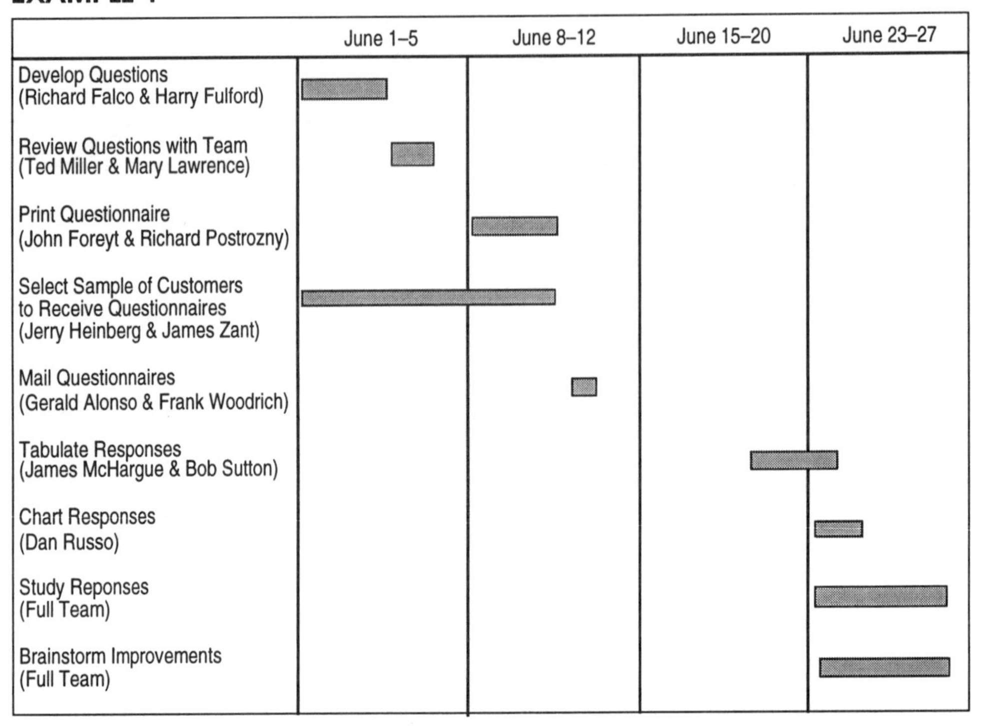

EXAMPLE 2

Item #	Activity	Responsible Persons	Due Date	Budget	Report to:
	Develop Questions	Richard Falco & Harry Fulford	6/3/97		ISA
	Review Questions with Team	Ted Miller & Mary Lawrence	6/5/97		ISA
	Print Questionnaire	John Foreyt & Richard Postrozny	6/10/97	$1,942	ISA/VPA*
	Select Sample of Customers to Receive Questionnaires	Jerry Heinberg & James Zant	6/10/97		ISA
	Mail Questionnaires	Gerald Alonso & Frank Woodrich	6/12/97	$1,995	ISA/VPA
	Tabulate Responses	James McHargue & Bob Sutton	6/22/97		ISA
	Chart Responses	Dan Russo	6/25/97	$575	ISA/VPA
	Study Responses	Full Team	6/27/97		ISA
	Brainstorm Improvements	Full Team	6/27/97		ISA

*This chart suggests that "VPA" has something to do with finance, because that office must have information whenever money is spent.

15 NOMINAL GROUP TECHNIQUE

Earlier, we discussed the subject of "brainstorming" and concluded that it is a technique frequently used by teams seeking solutions. If you have not studied brainstorming yet, this would be a good time to go back and do so. The technique known as "nominal group" is one that builds on the brainstorming idea and represents a highly structured approach to generating ideas.

WHAT IS IT?

The **Nominal Group Technique (NGT)** is a way to help a small group or team of people survey and clarify their thoughts concerning an issue. Furthermore, NGT helps the team prioritize the list of concerns, opinions or possible ideas to study. It is often used to select a process to study an improvement effort, for an end result of NGT is consensus by team members as to what they consider important. Support to address the process is thus assured. Note that this form of selecting a process to study differs from suggestions from management or customers, and may not have as much data readily available. The word "nominal" is used because NGT involves nominal discussion vs. open, unregulated discussion in other brainstorming techniques.

"Multivoting" is another similar technique; however, it differs from NGT in one important way. Multivoting involves taking multiple votes by a team to rank or narrow a list of concerns, opinions or possible areas to study. The multiple voting is done *as a group*, whereas NGT involves private decision-making with restricted interaction by group members.

WHY SHOULD IT BE USED?

The Nominal Group Technique is an excellent way to produce a wealth of ideas very rapidly. NGT places its focus on the identification and ranking of concerns, opinions or possible ideas to study, and opens communication by insuring that all members participate. Everyone has an opportunity to contribute and is actually forced to contribute and rank.

NGT is also very valuable as an aid when you are working with a larger group of people addressing conflicting ideas. For example, we once used NGT to identify, clarify, list and place in priority order the needs that should be presented to the legislature for our Legislative Budget Request (LBR). The participants in the room included customers of our services, vendors who provided services, parents of customers, legislators and their assistants, professional associates working for our agency, and managers. This was a most diverse group, with conflicting ideas concerning what should be requested in the LBR. Using NGT, we were able to set priorities that were accepted by the group. It was very difficult for any one particular participant to disagree with the democratic process that was open for all to see.

WHAT DOES A TEAM NEED TO USE IT?

The primary need is a good understanding of the process of NGT. This can be accomplished by having a good facilitator who is knowledgeable and skilled. Also needed is a supply of flip charts and markers, masking tape, and a supply of paper for individuals to write their ideas.

HOW DO WE DO IT? WHAT ARE THE RULES?

Refer back to the earlier discussion on brainstorming, because so much of NGT depends upon a good understanding of that technique. The basic steps in NGT follow.

Step One

The leader or facilitator explains the topic, process or problem that will be discussed by the group. An explanation of Nominal Group Technique is provided, along with the rules and procedures that will be followed. It is important that everyone accept these guidelines and agree to follow the process by actively participating.

Step Two

The leader or facilitator reads the topic, process or problem that will be discussed. This can take the form of a question. For example, *What should the Legislative Budget Request contain for Fiscal Year 96-97?*

This topic, process or problem should then be written on one of the flip charts for all to see and refer to as necessary. Although no discussion should be allowed at this point, it is necessary that everyone understand what is being discussed. For example, does everyone understand what a Legislative Budget Request is and what is meant by Fiscal Year?

Step Three

The group is now allowed ten minutes to generate ideas. Each person should do this alone with no discussion. Each idea should be written down by individuals on their own sheet of paper. Those who finish early should just sit quietly until the ten minutes passes. No one should be allowed to get up, talk to their neighbor or distract in any manner those who are still thinking. This step is critical to the technique of NGT.

Step Four

The leader now goes around the group gathering ideas from each participant. One idea at a time is provided by each member and then written on one of the flip charts. When everyone has given the leader their first idea, a second round takes place with each participant's second idea listed on the flip chart. The leader's flip chart might look like this:

LBR 96-97 NEEDS

- More funding for evaluation
- More training resources
- More training
- Better transportation
- Mental health counseling
- Better counselors (more pay)
- Faster services
- Improved funding
- Fewer delays
- More evaluation
- Buses
- Counseling

No discussion is allowed here, just the ideas. All the ideas are listed until there are no more left by any participant. The list may be several pages long, with lots of duplication. That is acceptable.

Step Five

With the flip charts in full view, the leader or facilitator leads a discussion of the ideas generated. Ideas are clarified by those who proposed them, and some are combined. In a large group there will undoubtedly be a great deal of duplication. The idea here is to clarify each idea so that there is no misunderstanding concerning it by anyone in the room. This is not the time for deep discussion, philosophical arguments, etc. Consider the following:

- Mental Health Counseling
- Counseling

To many participants these two subjects appear the same and should be combined. Yet, in the minds of others, there might be a great deal of difference between what is meant by "mental health counseling" and "counseling," which might involve career or vocational counseling.

Focus on clarification of meaning, not the number of suggestions.

Step Six

This is where participants decide what items they consider most important. Each participant rank orders the ideas by assigning a score to each. If there are many ideas, it is acceptable to try to bring the list down a bit by asking the group to remove some of the "less critical" through simple multivoting. In other words, the facilitator might say something like:

> All of us know that we will never be able to place all 75 of these needs in the Legislative Budget Request. Would you feel comfortable in voting your top twenty-five? Then we will narrow down that list and place it in order of importance later."

The final list is then written by the facilitator or leader on another flip chart. It might look like this:

- More funding for evaluation
- More training resources
- Better transportation
- Mental health counseling
- Better counseling with better pay

Once the list is narrowed, if necessary, each participant places the list in the order they think is most important. This is done quietly without discussion, following the same rules contained in Step Three. In the example above, participants would assign a "5" to the most important item, and a "1" to the least important. Five minutes are allowed for this analysis. Anyone finishing early should merely sit quietly until the others are done.

Step Seven

The votes for each item are tabulated. At this point, it is possible to "take the vote" in a variety of ways. Much is dependent upon the size of the group, the number of ideas and the leader's or facilitator's desires. You may merely ask group members to call out their votes and then tally the numbers after everyone is finished.

Another approach is to hand out round, colored dot stickers you can purchase at any office supply store. Give each participant a sufficient supply of red, blue, yellow, green, etc. stickers and assign a weight to each. Then ask participants to vote by placing their appropriate "dots" right on the flip chart. It is a relatively easy thing to count the stickers to tally the vote. An added benefit is that participants can get up and stretch a bit as they vote.

Step Eight

Once the vote is in, it is acceptable to take a few minutes to discuss the results. It is possible to construct, on the spot, a Pareto chart to display the results. The group may then wish to convene again to develop an action plan based upon the results.

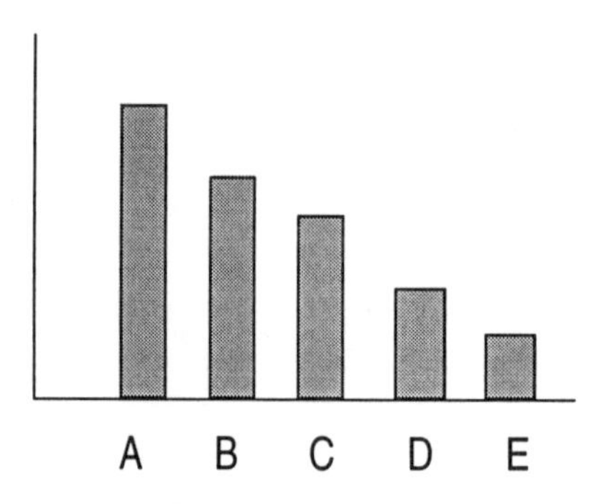

A - Better transportation

B - More training resources

C - More funding for evaluation

D - Mental health counseling

E - Better counseling with better pay

16 PARETO CHARTS

Joseph Juran, one of the prominent "gurus" of quality improvement noted that only a few factors contributing to an effect actually account for the bulk of the effect. In other words, you may have fourteen factors causing a problem, but three of those account for 80% of the problem.

To resolve the problem, it would be wise to address the three major causes of trouble before looking at the remaining eleven. In other words, hunt ducks where the ducks are. Juran called this observation, that a few factors cause the bulk, the "Pareto" principle. Actually, Pareto was an economist who noted that a relatively small number of people (20%) controlled most of the wealth in Italy (80%).

There are many examples of the "80–20" rule in our own lives. It is often said that 20% of our customers in government take 80% of our time, and the other 80% take only 20% of our time. Think of your own experience. If you are a direct-service provider, you may recall the few difficult customers that really needed tremendous assistance in finding a job, dealing with everyday problems, etc. On the other hand, the bulk (80%) of your customers were "in and out" of your office very quickly. Supervisors note that a small number of those they supervise take up far more time than the others who need little guidance and supervision.

The **Pareto chart** helps us clarify those problems that should be addressed first.

WHAT IS IT?

The Pareto chart is a bar chart that distinguishes the "important" from the "not-so-important" when examining data. The bars appear in rank order, with the bar on the left showing the greatest number of observations, and the bar on the far right showing the least. A curved line across the top of the graph shows the cumulative percentages so that it is relatively easy to see what factors contribute to 45%, 75% or 90% of the problem under study.

The Pareto chart is fairly easy to construct and because of its value is one of the most popular tools used by quality teams.

WHY SHOULD IT BE USED?

The Pareto chart helps the team concentrate on those factors that are most important. It is relatively easy to be overcome by a multitude of causes and waste time looking at minor issues when working on a problem. For example, when we were discussing Nominal Group Technique, we identified the following needs for the Legislative Budget Request:

More funding for evaluation

More training resources

Better transportation

Mental health counseling

Better counseling with better pay

When the vote was taken, we found that 15 people said that "better transportation" was the most critical issue; 13 said "more training resources" was important; 10 wanted "more funding for evaluation"; 7 voted for "mental health counseling"; and 5 said that "better counseling with better pay" was important. By placing these numbers in a Pareto chart, it is possible to demonstrate clearly how important each issue is and which one should be addressed first.

WHAT DOES A TEAM NEED TO USE IT?

The Pareto chart is an easy chart to construct. The calculations are kept to a minimum, and the only things needed are a basic understanding of the tool, the data, some paper, a ruler, and a pencil. A calculator will help with the percentages, but is not absolutely necessary.

HOW DO WE DO IT? WHAT ARE THE RULES?

These steps are suggestions only. There are no concrete rules for constructing Pareto charts.

Step One

List all the factors that were observed. In some cases, these are the factors causing the problem to exist that the team found in their brainstorming or data collection.

Let us construct a Pareto chart that will help define and clarify those factors that cause a problem for most of us. This is an example that we use regularly in our training seminars and clearly shows how to construct the chart.

The problem identified is Money Problems. Here are the factors that the team listed as probable causes of the problem.

Money Problems

Child care expenses

Food

Rent/mortgage

Health insurance

Home insurance

Auto insurance

Children (school expenses, clothing, etc.)

We have a good beginning in examining our problem. However, even with this list we have little idea of the how important each factor is, and which we should examine in more detail. In other words, is the first factor listed, "child care expenses," more important than "auto insurance?"

If we asked all participants in the class to identify the number one problem that they had with money at a given moment, what would it be?

Step Two

Measure relevant factors. This is where it is necessary to gather data. If you are examining the reasons why your customers use the telephone to contact your office, you categorize (as we just did above) and then count the number of times a call fits into that category. Note that these totals are valid just for the time during which the data is taken. It may change the next day and probably will. Be careful when you collect the data, for data collected at the end of the week or month may be significantly different than at other times.

In our example, we merely asked each of the members of the class to hold up their hands if they thought the factor was the number one reason why they were having current money problems. In counting hands, we found the following:

Money Problems

Child care expenses	14
Food	42
Rent/mortgage	26
Health insurance	58
Home insurance	16
Auto insurance	28
Children	16

Most participants' money problems resulted from the high cost of health insurance. However, given the data in its current form, it is still somewhat difficult to visualize how much each factor contributes to the whole.

Step Three

Make a table showing the rank order of categories from highest to lowest.

Factor	Number	%	Cumulative %
Health insurance	58		
Food	42		
Auto insurance	28		
Rent/mortgage	26		
Home insurance	16		
Children (school expenses, clothing, etc.)	16		
Child care expenses	14		

Step Four

Calculate the percentage and the cumulative percentage for each factor. To do this, total the number of responses, and divide this number into each of the individual response numbers. In our example we had a total of 200 votes. In the first factor ("Health insurance") we divide 200 into 58 to come up with .29, or 29%.

Factor	Number	%	Cumulative %
Health insurance	58	29	29
Food	42	21	50
Auto insurance	28	14	64
Rent/mortgage	26	13	77
Home insurance	16	8	85
Children (school expenses, clothing, etc.)	16	8	93
Child care expenses	14	7	100

Without even constructing a Pareto chart, organization of data in a chart (as shown above) helps identify factors that are more important than others. For example, two factors ("Health insurance" and "Food") account for half (50%) of the votes. If a team examined these two (which account for only two out of seven listed), they would be addressing one-half of the major factors identified by the group. Had they selected the last two (Children and Child care expenses), they might spend just as much time addressing these, representing only 15% of the factors identified by the group.

Step Five

The next step is to construct the chart (see example top of next page).

a. Begin by drawing a **left vertical axis** that is equal to the total number of measurements taken. In our example, this axis will be equal to the 200 votes counted.

b. Then draw a **right vertical axis** the same length as the left one that will represent the percentage of each factor.

Step Six

Our next step is to take the data in our table and draw bars to represent each category. Often the bars will be labeled in a narrative fashion directly under the bar. We will code the factors "A" through "G" and provide an explanation with a key (see example bottom of next page).

This completes the first portion of our Pareto chart, and in fact, many people do not go beyond this point. An examination of the heights of the various bars provides an excellent graphical representation of the extent of each factor and its contribution to the whole. For example, in our unfinished Pareto chart (minus the percentages, which will be covered in the ***Step Seven***), we see that "Health insurance" is a far more serious money problem than is "Child care expenses" in this observation. The same might not be true

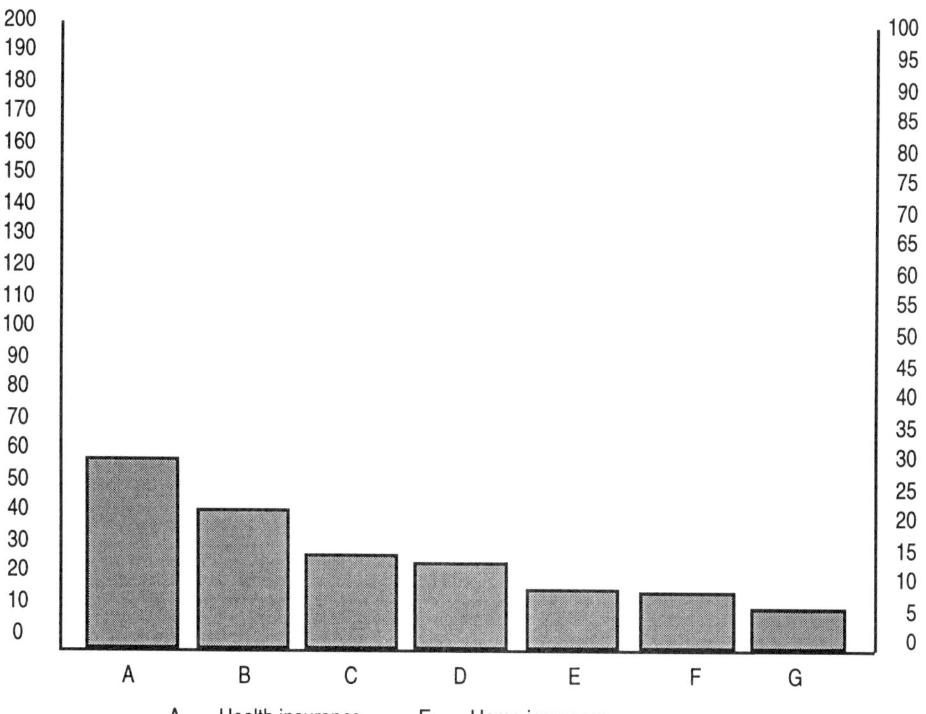

A - Health insurance
B - Food
C - Auto insurance
D - Rent/mortgage
E - Home insurance
F - Children (school expenses, clothing, etc.)
G - Child care expenses

with another set of observations with different people. If the room was filled with millionaires, it is likely that something like a "declining stock market" or "travel to Europe" might be highly ranked while "Health insurance" may not even being mentioned. The importance of careful selection of original data cannot be overemphasized.

Factor	Number	%	Cumulative %
Health insurance	58	29	29
Food	42	21	50
Auto insurance	28	14	64
Rent/mortgage	26	13	77
Home insurance	16	8	85
Children (school expenses, clothing, etc.)	16	8	93
Child care expenses	14	7	100

COMPLETE PARETO CHART

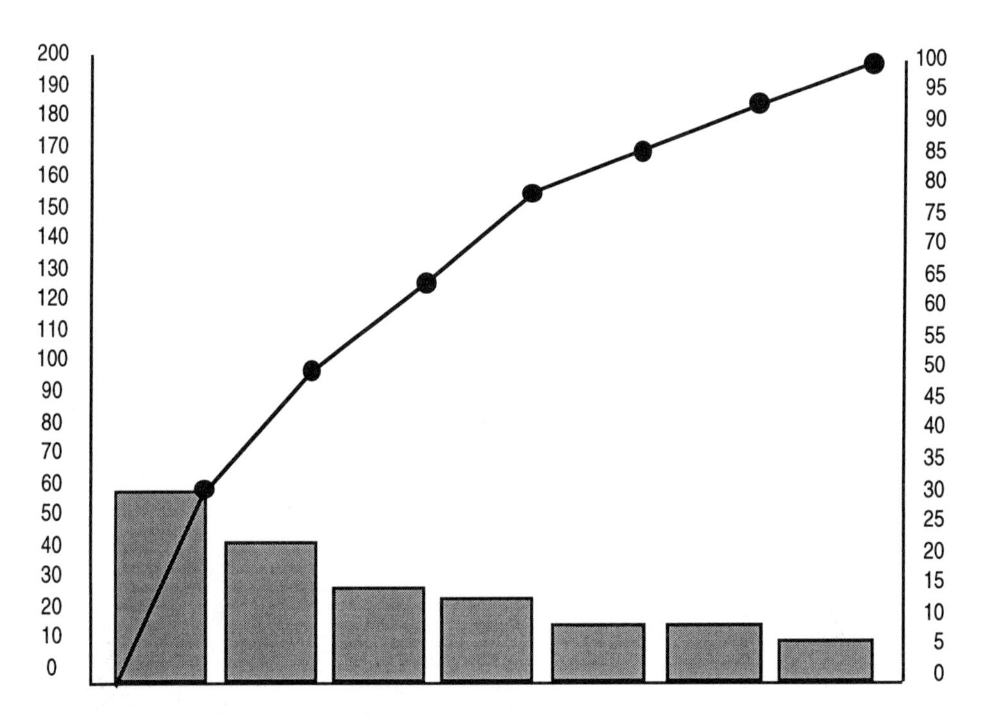

A - Health insurance
B - Food
C - Auto insurance
D - Rent/mortgage
E - Home insurance
F - Children (school expenses, clothing, etc.)
G - Child care expenses

STEP SEVEN

Now plot the cumulative percentages for the Pareto chart. Take the percentage for each factor and place a dot on the Pareto chart either on the bar or above it depending upon where it "falls." In our example, the first dot (for "Health insurance") falls at the 29% level. The dot is *actually right on the top* of the bar. The dot is placed on the right hand corner to allow the line to begin at the bottom left corner where the reading is "0." The second dot falls at the 50% level, and we place the dot above the "Food" bar, about where the right side would be if the bar went up that far. Do the same for the remaining cumulative percentages and then merely connect the dots (see example previous page).

INTERPRETATIONS

The previous chart under ***Step Seven*** is a complete Pareto chart. With the addition of the cumulative percentage "dots" and the connecting line, we have a chart that can tell us a great deal.

The chart below is the *same* Pareto chart, except that we have added a few lines and notes to show what can be interpreted from the original chart.

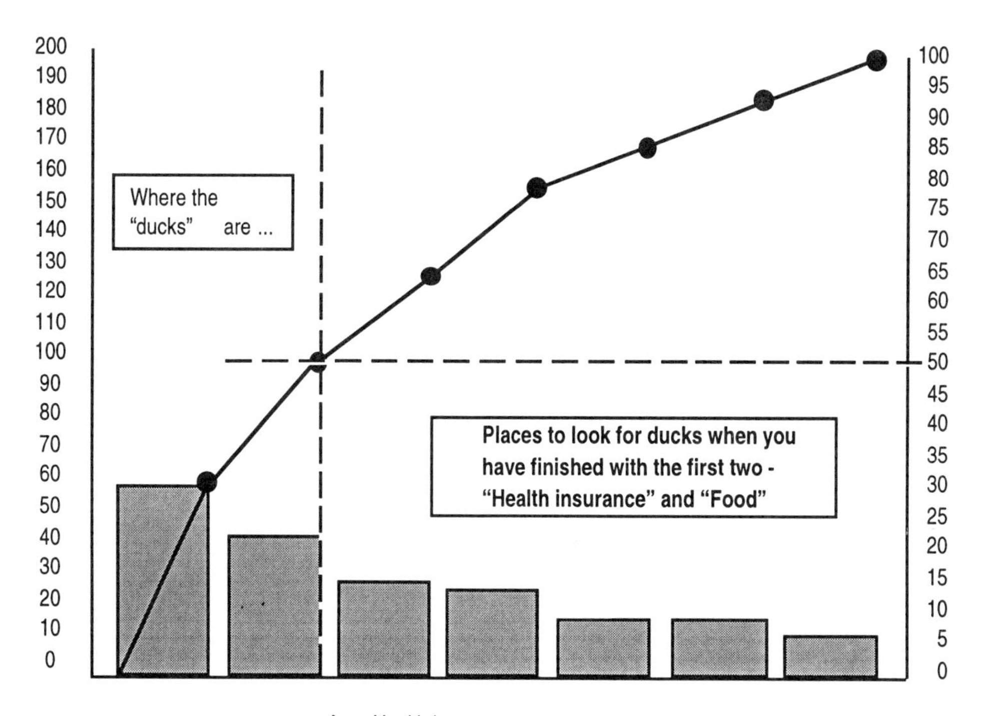

A - Health insurance
B - Food
C - Auto insurance
D - Rent/mortgage
E - Home insurance
F - Children (school expenses, clothing, etc.)
G - Child care expenses

INTERPRETATIONS

So what conclusions can be reached after studying this chart? You may come up with other interpretations; however, we suggest the following:

- The team addressing money problems would be wise to concentrate on the first two factors. These two, out of a total of seven, account for 50% of the votes. It is obvious that the cost of health insurance and food is a major problem. (These are where "the ducks" are.) The team may begin to address the health insurance problem by suggesting the development of a healthier lifestyle with fewer trips requiring co-payments, investigation of different health plans, etc. The cost of food may be reduced by eating out less often, shopping for specials, purchasing less prepared food, etc.
- This example produced a "rather flat" Pareto chart. Perhaps we did not get valid data or did not ask the question properly. Certainly there may be more categories (like recreation and transportation). *Most* Pareto charts will look like the following example.

EXAMPLE OF A "MORE TYPICAL" PARETO CHART

Chances are good that many of the charts you produce will demonstrate that 80% of most problems will be the result of less than 20% of causes, as shown in the chart below.

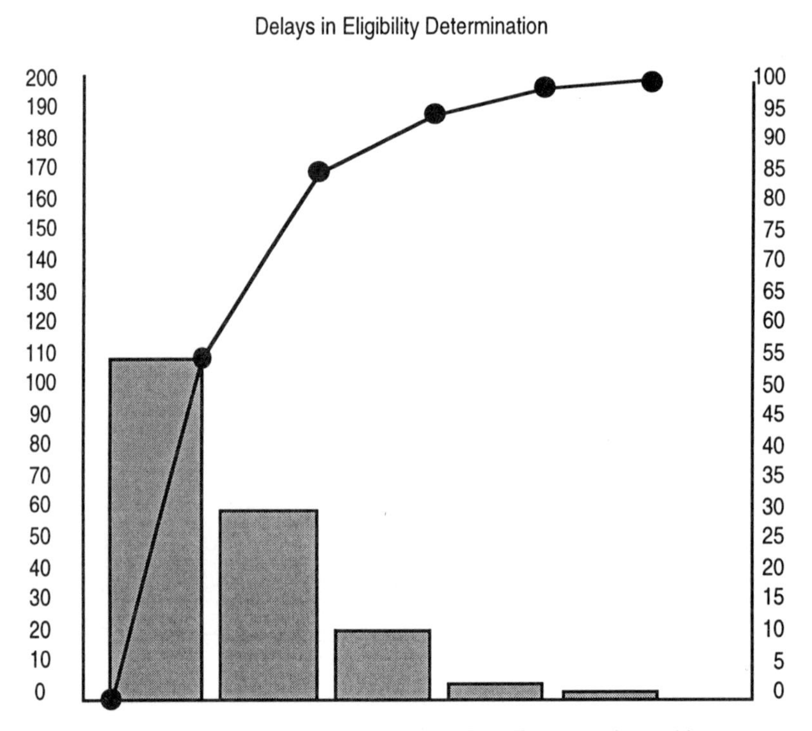

With the information provided by the above Pareto chart, a team addressing an improvement in eligibility determination in vocational rehabilitation would be well advised to concentrate on the first two reasons. These two account for over 80% of the problem.

AN ACTUAL PARETO CHART FROM UNEMPLOYMENT COMPENSATION

One of the best Pareto charts we have seen appears below. The chart was developed by an Unemployment Compensation Appeals Information Team in West Palm Beach, Florida and is actually *two Pareto charts* in one! Note that this team charted the reasons why telephone calls were placed to their office by customers. On the left hand side of this chart are the calls made during the period 9/20/93 to 10/1/93. On the right hand side are the calls placed to the office *after* the process improvements were made by the team.

The team suggested that instructions provided in the initial letter sent to the customer also include a "Map to Our Office." The Pareto chart shows the impact of the suggestion, as well as providing thought and direction for future improvement efforts.

Note: (1) The dramatic reduction in the number of calls asking for "Directions," and (2) the also dramatic increase in requests for "Claims information." Customers could now reach the office for this information, because the telephone lines were not tied up with people asking for directions to the office!

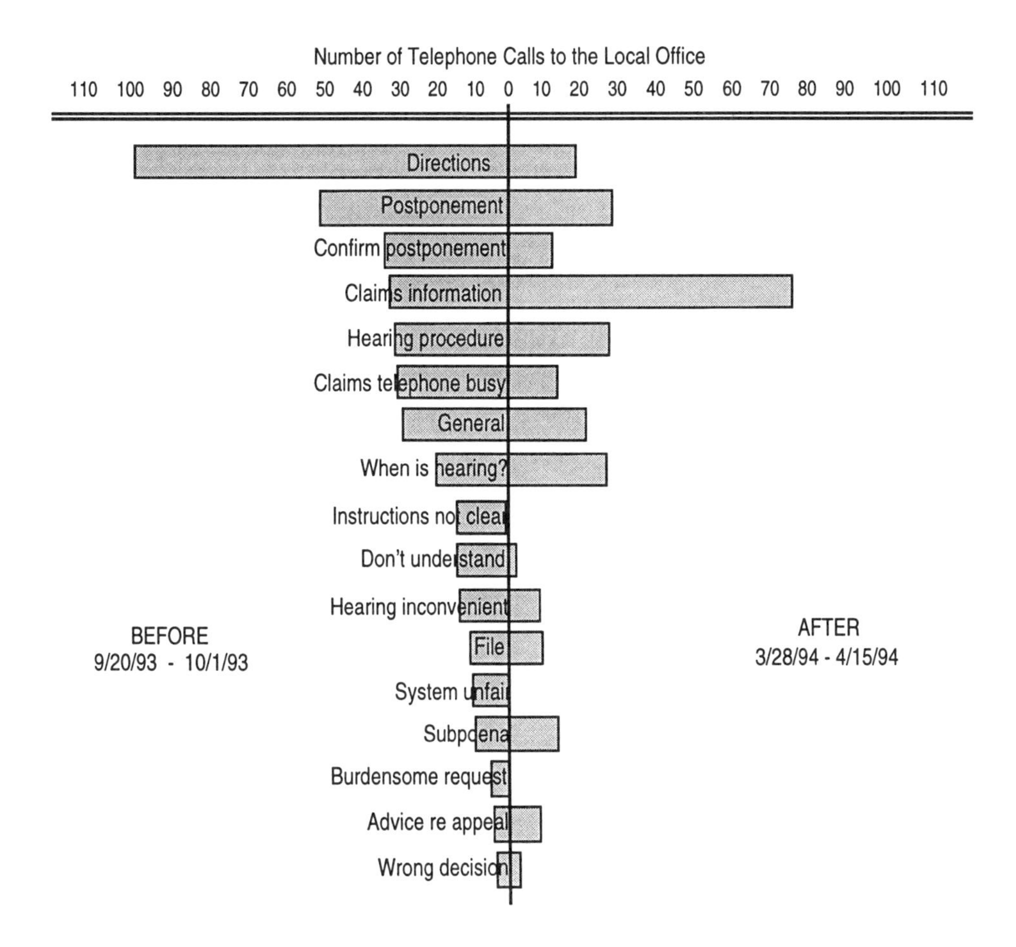

BLUE CHIPS

- The Pareto chart is a very versatile tool. It can be used throughout the continual improvement process. First, we can use a Pareto chart to help decide which problem to study first ("Go where the ducks are..."). Then, after we have selected the problem to study, we can again use the Pareto chart to determine which causes of the problem are the ones we should tackle.
- The Pareto chart helps the team handle emotional judgments and presumptions. Someone may say that he knows exactly what is causing a problem and refuses to consider other causes. When actual data is gathered and used in a Pareto chart, he may be proven right or he may be wrong, but the facts will be available.

Juran in his *Quality Control Handbook,* makes the following observations about Pareto charts:

Generally, people hold strong opinions on what are the important areas requiring attention, but these opinions are often not shared by others. The Pareto concept helps to achieve agreement by collecting facts and summarizing them in a form that shows where most of the problem is concentrated.

17 PIE CHARTS

Pie Charts are probably the most familiar tool that is occasionally used by teams. The reason why they are not used more often is that their value, compared to the amount of work required to draw one, does not measure up to the other tools available. The same information can be shown on a Pareto chart with greater understanding, as demonstrated below.

WHAT IS IT?

The **Pie Chart** is a simple circle that represents 100% of the data collected.

WHY SHOULD IT BE USED?

The Pie Chart shows graphically the relationships among parts of a whole. The major reason a team may wish to use it is that popular computer software programs, like Microsoft's EXCEL, will automatically compute the numbers and construct colorful pie charts with little effort.

HOW DO WE DO IT? WHAT ARE THE RULES?

The steps to construct a Pie Chart are:

Step One

Decide what categories will be used and collect the data.

Step Two

Calculate the percentages for each category, and illustrate these percentages as slices of the pie.

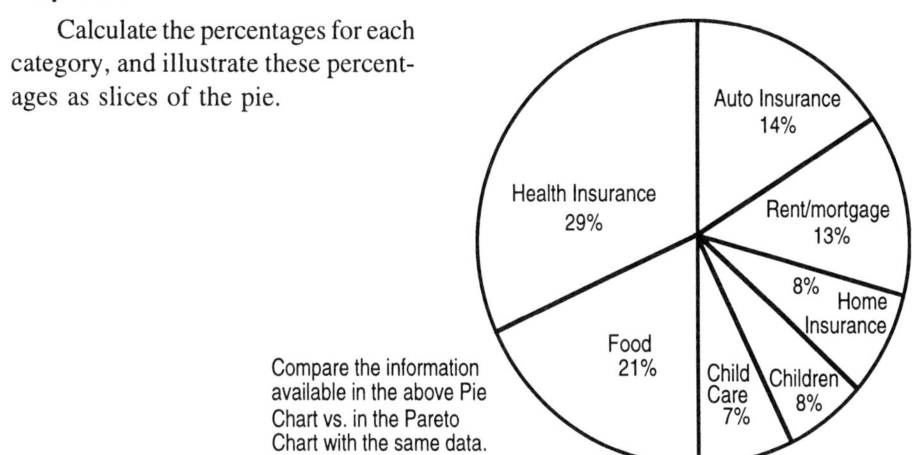

Compare the information available in the above Pie Chart vs. in the Pareto Chart with the same data.

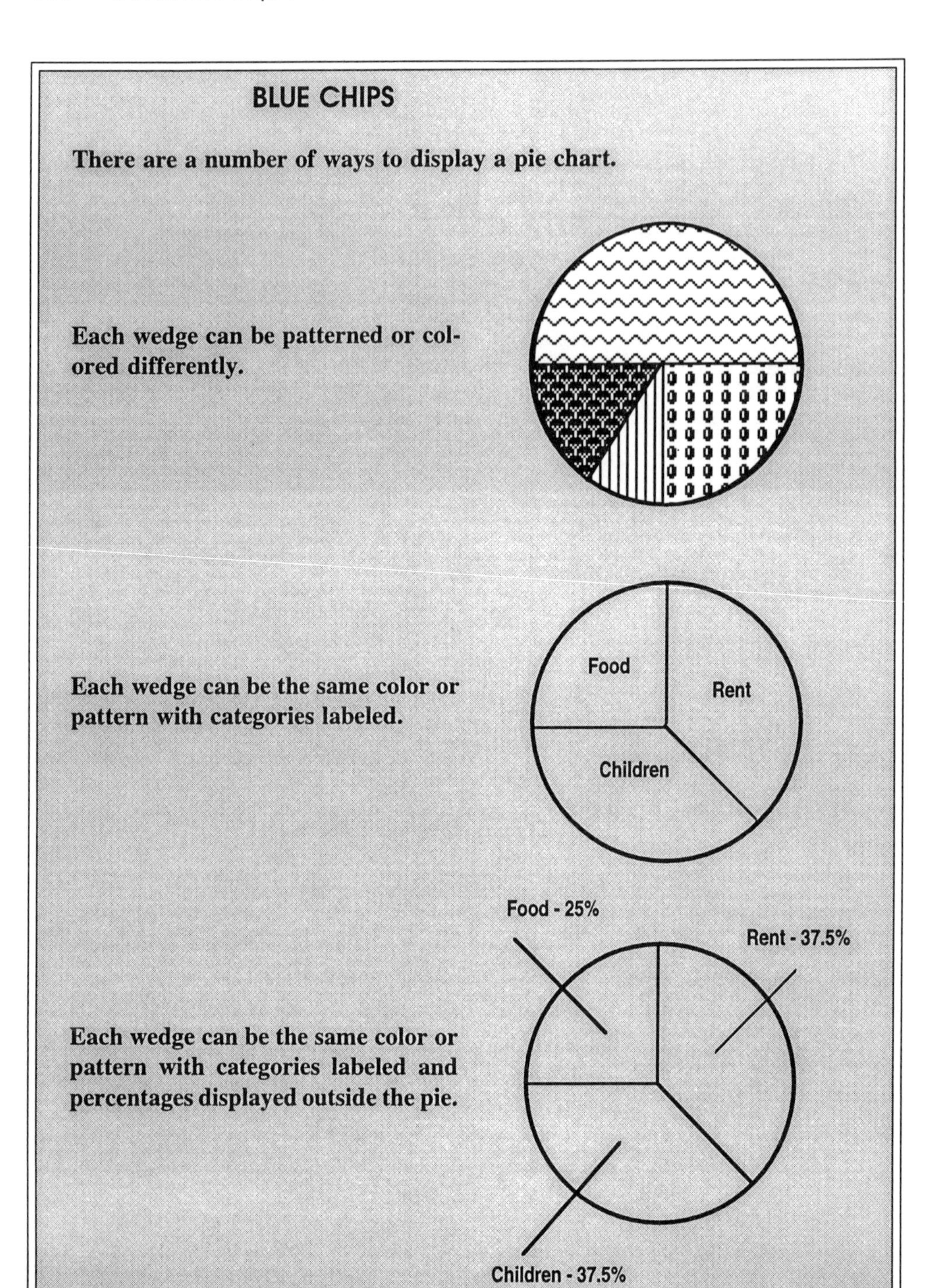

BLUE CHIPS

There are a number of ways to display a pie chart.

Each wedge can be patterned or colored differently.

Each wedge can be the same color or pattern with categories labeled.

Each wedge can be the same color or pattern with categories labeled and percentages displayed outside the pie.

18 PRIORITY SELECTION WORKSHEETS

The **Priority Selection Worksheet** is a tool that is very useful when a team finds that they have more than they can possibly do. Although somewhat depressing at times, there are numerous problems that teams uncover when they begin examining their processes. In fact, it is not unusual for a team to decide to do nothing, given the magnitude and number of problems uncovered in their deliberations.

When this happens, turn to the Priority Selection Worksheet. A copy of the worksheet is provided here that may be duplicated on a copier.

WHAT IS IT?

The Priority Selection Worksheet is another way for the team to decide the relative priorities of the issues they might address. Recall that priorities when can also be examined with the Nominal Group Technique. It is nice to have a wealth of tools available.

WHY SHOULD IT BE USED?

The Priority Selection Worksheet enables teams to arrive at a consensus relative to the importance of problems they face. They can then proceed with the solution.

WHAT DOES A TEAM NEED TO USE IT?

The worksheet, a pencil, and a desire to attack the most serious issues first.

HOW DO WE DO IT? WHAT ARE THE RULES?

Step One

Through brainstorming or other techniques, generate a list of problems that may be addressed by the team.

Step Two

This is probably the most important. The team needs to agree upon what evaluation criteria will be used on the worksheet.

Examples of criteria can include:

- Do we have the resources to resolve the problem?
- How much would it cost to resolve?
- Will management be receptive to our study of the problem?
- How important is this problem to our customers?

- How much time will the study of the problem take?
- Can we measure the results of improvement?

Step Three

Construct a grid with the measurement criteria along the vertical axis and the potential problems along the horizontal axis. When we were discussing **Cause and Effect Diagrams**, we saw an example that identified a number of potential problems that were contributing to "excessive waiting time" for customers in the Department of Labor and Employment Security. Let us use these problems in our worksheet.

		Counters Lack Organization	Staff Stressed Out	Insufficient Training Materials	Not Enough Computer Terminals	Insufficient Permanent Staff
Resources Available?	Yes = 5					
Cost to Correct?	Low = 5					
Management Receptivity?	High = 5					
Importance to Customer	High = 5					
Time to Correct	Short = 5					
Can We Measure Results?	Yes = 5					
	Total Points					

Step Four

Each member of the team takes a copy of the form and individually ranks each problem in accordance with the criteria agreed upon by the team. Note that each criteria has a code within the worksheet that helps them define their score. In each instance the "good" response is a "5," and the "poor" response is a "0."

After a team member completes his form, it might appear as follows:

		Counters Lack Organization	Staff Stressed Out	Insufficient Training Materials	Not Enough Computer Terminals	Insufficient Permanent Staff
Resources Available?	Yes = 5	*5*	*2*	*1*	*1*	*1*
Cost to Correct?	Low = 5	*5*	*2*	*2*	*1*	*1*
Management Receptivity?	High = 5	*5*	*5*	*4*	*4*	*5*
Importance to Customer	High = 5	*5*	*5*	*5*	*5*	*5*
Time to Correct	Short = 5	*5*	*3*	*2*	*3*	*1*
Can We Measure Results?	Yes = 5	*5*	*4*	*4*	*5*	*4*
	Total Points	*30*	*21*	*18*	*19*	*17*

When all the points are totaled, the team selects for study the one with the highest total.

PRIORITY SELECTION WORKSHEET

Name of Team__________________
Date ______________

Problems

Measurement Criteria				
Total Points				

WHERE DO WE FIND THE PROBLEMS?

On occasion, teams actually get stuck in the early stages of their work when they draw a blank on where to look for problems. They would use a priority selection worksheet if and when they locate a problem.

If the team has trouble locating problems, ask the following questions.

- Where are customers complaining about the process?
- Where are mistakes being made?
- Where do supervisors from headquarters look when they examine your work?
- Are there any unnecessary reports due each month?
- Do you ever have to do something over again?
- Are there ever any arguments or differences of opinion about how your office should work?
- Is office morale ever low? Do associates appear dissatisfied?
- Is anyone in your office ever confused about some policy?
- Is absenteeism a problem in your office?
- Do you ever see anyone waiting in line at your office?
- Has anyone ever said "If they would just let us..."
- Is there a high turnover in any of your positions?
- Do people like working in your office?

19 RUN CHARTS

One of the easiest, yet most useful tools for a team to use in its process improvements is the **Run Chart**. Perhaps because it is so easy to construct, teams think that it may not be useful. Nothing could be farther from the truth, and as with all tools, the Run Chart has its place.

WHAT IS IT?

Sometimes called a Trend Chart, the Run Chart helps track data over a specific time period and enables the team to spot patterns or trends. This chart can also be used to spot unusual events or to continuously monitor performance. Run charts are very common and appear in daily publications, such as those on the financial pages which show the rise and fall of the stock market.

A central line in the chart provides the mean or average.

WHY SHOULD IT BE USED?

The primary use for the Run Chart by a quality improvement team would be to understand what is happening in the process under study. For example, if waiting time in lines is under study, a run chart listing the average times in a line at various times during the day would provide data on when customers are likely to come in for services. The chart will show increasing or decreasing trends, and may assist the team in potential process changes.

WHAT DOES A TEAM NEED TO USE IT?

The primary requirement is basic understanding of the uses for the chart, data, a pencil, paper, and ruler. The only statistic involved is the calculation of the average, also called the mean.

HOW DO WE DO IT? WHAT ARE THE RULES?

Step One

Decide what you wish to track. This is easier than it sounds. Make certain that the data directly relates to the process you are studying and that it is important to the customer. How difficult will it be to collect the data? Is the data already available elsewhere (like the mainframe computer)? Who will collect the data?

Step Two

Collect the data. It is helpful to store the data in a table until the chart is constructed. As an example, we will track the number of customers seeking services over a one week period. The following data was collected for the third week in November:

Day of Week	Number of Customers
Monday	57
Tuesday	46
Wednesday	43
Thursday	45
Friday	23

Step Three

Using the data gathered, begin constructing the Run Chart by placing the unit of measurement on the vertical axis, with the smallest number at the bottom. Use the horizontal axis for the days of the week. The horizontal axis represents time and never varies in a Run Chart. The time may be in seconds, minutes, hours, days, weeks, months, years, etc. The purpose of the Run Chart is to show trends or cycles over time.

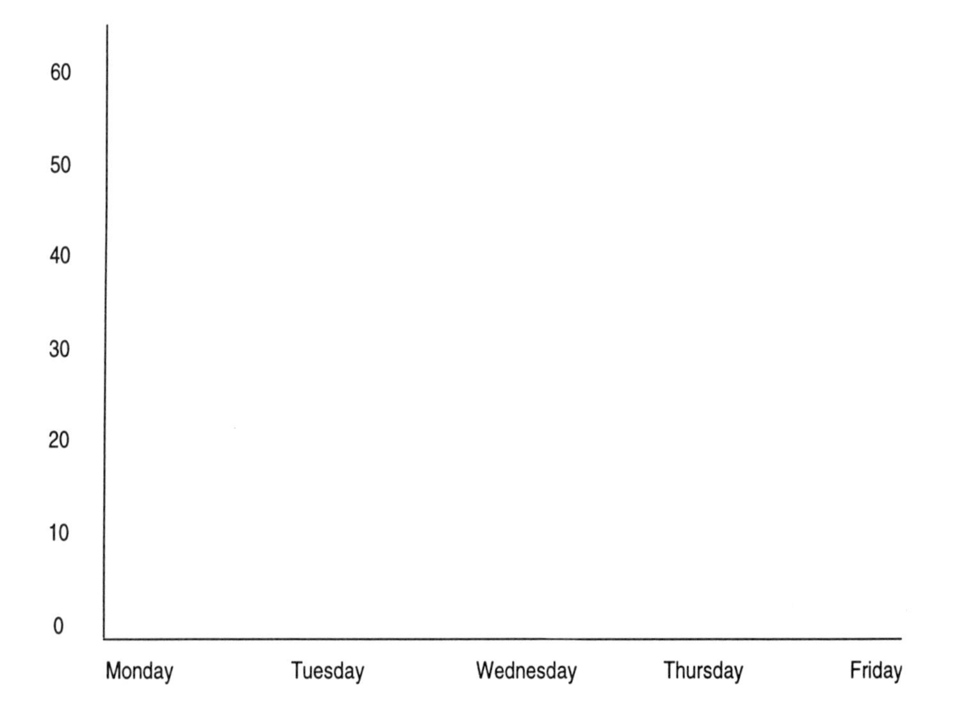

Step Four

Calculate the average (or mean) by adding the data and dividing by the number of observations taken. In our example above:

Average	**= Monday + Tuesday + Wednesday + Thursday + Friday / 5**
	= **57** **46** **43** **45** **23** **/ 5**
	= **42.8**

Step Five

Place a horizontal line representing the average or mean on the chart.

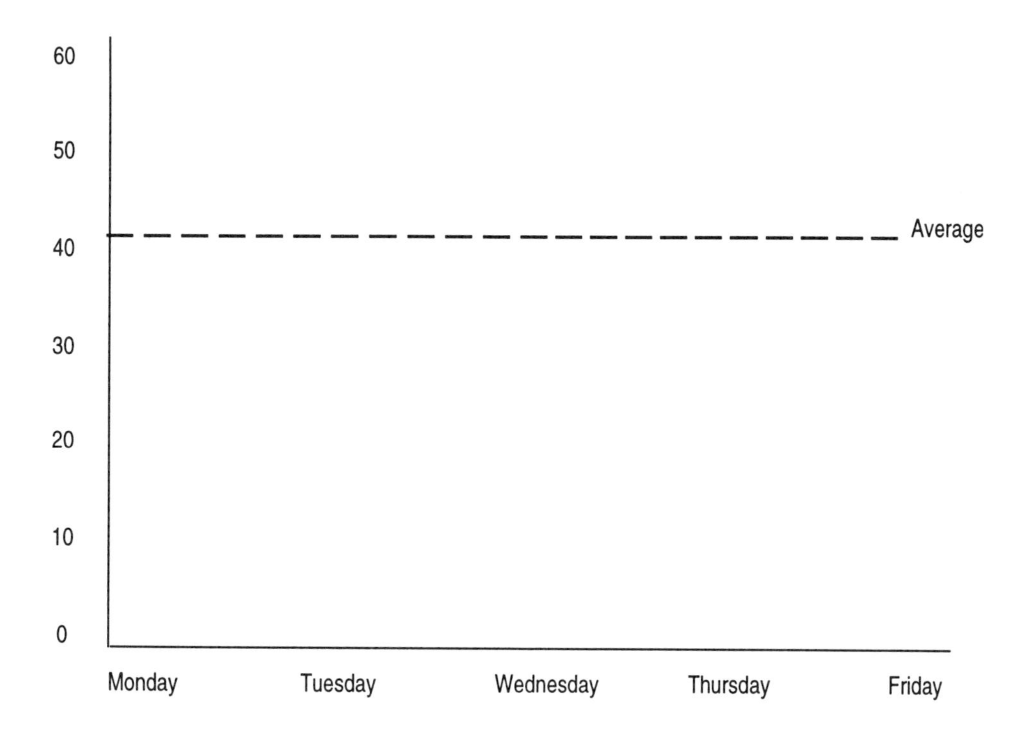

Step Six

Plot your data on the chart and connect the dots. This is the finished Run Chart.

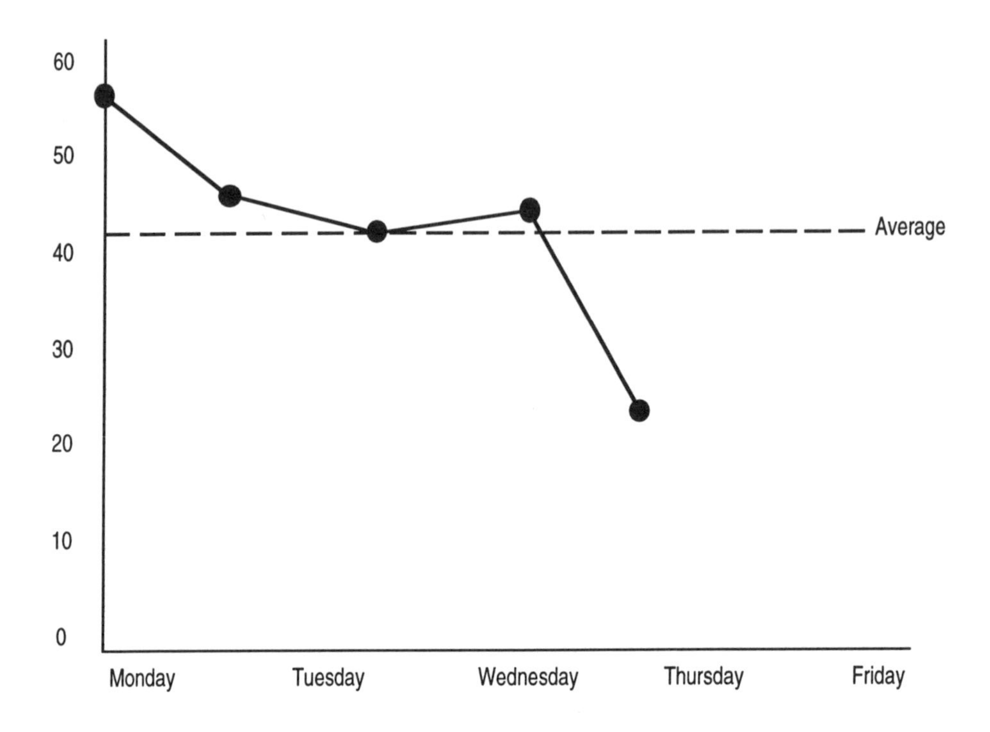

ANALYSIS

What can we tell from the Run Chart above?

This is a simple a Run Chart. Still, it does suggest that something unusual is going on. What accounts for the high number of customers on Monday vs. the low number on Friday?

The data is not sufficient to determine the reason for the high and low. There are only five entries covering one week. A trend or pattern cannot be determined for one week. Maybe it was raining all day Friday. Maybe Monday was the first day the office was open after a long holiday weekend. More data would be required for a valid Run Chart. Let's take data for a *full* month.

Monday, May 1	**57**	**Monday, May 15**	**48**	**Monday, May 29**	**0**
Tuesday, May 2	**46**	**Tuesday, May 16**	**44**	**Tuesday, May 30**	**62**
Wednesday, May 3	**43**	**Wednesday, May 17**	**38**	**Wednesday, May 31**	**47**
Thursday, May 4	**45**	**Thursday, May 18**	**46**		
Friday, May 5	**23**	**Friday, May 19**	**31**		
Monday, May 8	**51**	**Monday, May 22**	**51**		
Tuesday, May 9	**47**	**Tuesday, May 23**	**41**		
Wednesday, May 10	**42**	**Wednesday, May 24**	**43**		
Thursday, May 11	**47**	**Thursday, May 25**	**39**		
Friday, May 12	**31**	**Friday, May 26**	**21**		

First, calculate the average by dividing the number of days of observation (23) into the total number of customers who came into the office during May (949). The average is 41.26. This is just a little bit lower than the average we saw for the one week previously considered (42.8).

Add the horizontal line for the average and put the new time dimension on the horizontal axis. The vertical axis remains essentially the same for our current example, *except* that we must add one more higher number (70) on the axis to accommodate the high reading on May 30th. We also have a new low on Monday, May 29th. What happened?

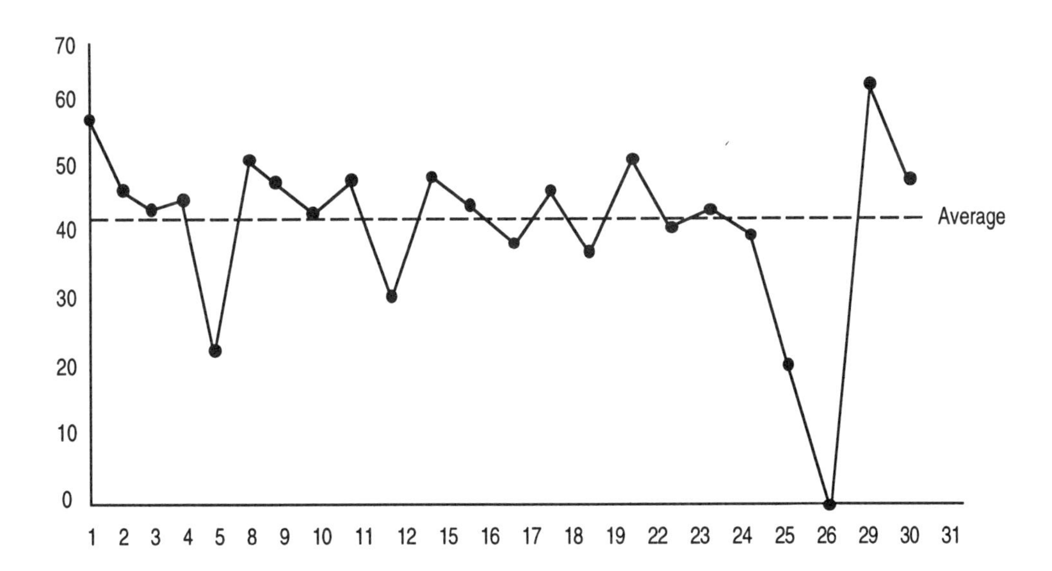

So, now we have our Run Chart for 23 days in May. There are a number of possible conclusions that might result from this data. Try your hand at analysis, given what little information you have, and list a few possibilities here. *After* you have given it a little thought, turn the page.

1.

2.

3.

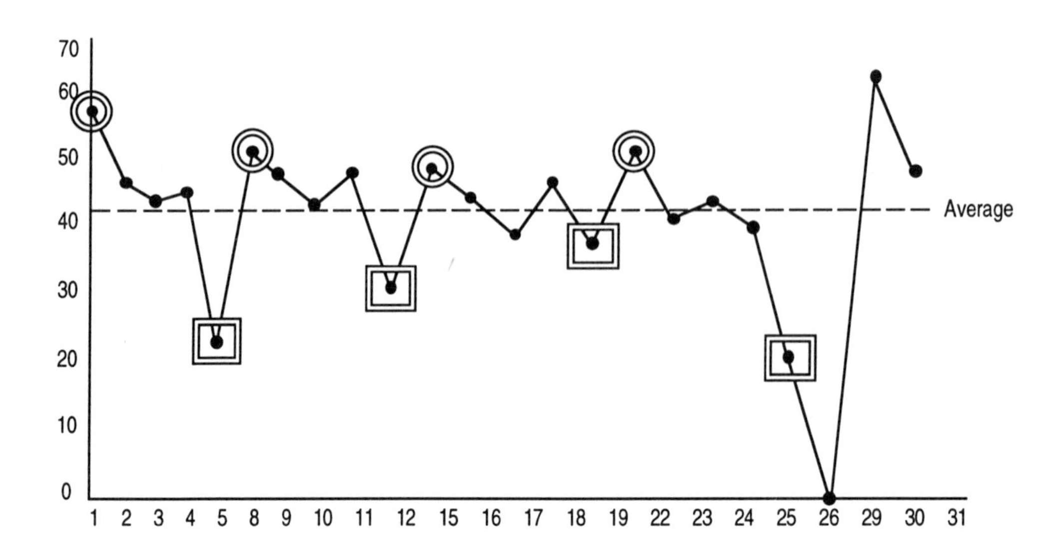

So what can we conclude? Your answers are probably as sound as ours, given the little information we have. See how they compare.

1. No real ongoing trends are readily apparent. On an average day about 40 customers arrive for services. There is no telling from this data what happened to them. Yet, these are potential customers, and another chart may show how many of them we helped find a job, get their teeth cleaned, etc. We are *not* seeing an increase or decrease in the number over a one-month period of time. It is a good bet that the month of June will look the same, unless we see an abundance of youngsters out of school for summer vacation looking for services.

2. Mondays are always the busiest, and Fridays the least busy. Note the ◎ circles we have placed on Mondays. Also note the Friday squares. ▢ This is a "trend" that the team may wish to address.

3. The above observations hold true except for Monday, May 29th. That happened to be Memorial Day when the office was closed. The customers "made up" for this the following day when a record number showed up. Always look for unusual circumstances in a Run Chart.

20 SCATTER DIAGRAMS

A few pages back, when we were discussing the **Cause and Effect diagram**, we mentioned a Japanese scientist, Dr. Kaoru Ishikawa, who was one of the first to use it. His book, *Guide to Quality Control,* is a classic work on quality. Dr. Ishikawa was also a great fan of the "Scatter Diagram," sometimes known as the "Scatterplot," and "Dot Plot."

WHAT IS IT?

The **Scatter Diagram** is a tool that is used to display the effects of one variable on another to determine the possible relationships between the variables. It is a graphic representation between two variables. However, just because a relationship appears, there is no guarantee that one causes the other. A classic example of this may be seen in the current debate concerning the relationship between violence on television and the increasing crime rate in the United States. Both have increased in the past ten years; however, there may be a number of factors contributing to the increase in crime. We have also seen an increase in the number of cellular telephones during this same time period, and if we used a scatter diagram to plot these two trends, we might be tempted to say that the increase in cellular telephone use contributed to the increase in crime.

WHY SHOULD IT BE USED?

The time to use a scatter diagram is when the team is questioning the "cause-effect" relationship between two variables and wishes to display this relationship.

WHAT DOES A TEAM NEED TO USE IT?

The primary requirement is a basic understanding of the uses for the chart, data, a pencil, paper, and ruler.

HOW DO WE DO IT? WHAT ARE THE RULES?

Step One

First, select the two variables to be compared. This is easier than it sounds. Make certain that the variables directly relate to the process you are studying and that any relationship established is important to the customer. All kinds of relationships are found in your work. Pick important potential linkages that you can influence through process improvements. Try to pick a relationship that team members have a "gut" feeling about, but have never investigated.

Step Two

Collect the data. It is helpful to store the data in a table until the chart is constructed. For our first example, we will track the average time it takes for a customer to be seen by a job services counselor and the number of successful placements made by an office. We will again store this data in a temporary table until we plot it.

Step Three

Place the data in the scatter diagram table.

Average Number of Minutes Taken to See Customer on First Visit	Average Number of Successful Job Placements/Month
34	490
44	427
42	480
37	466
55	370
61	341
48	410
42	472
49	383
55	351
43	444
39	482

This is good data. Still, it is not very easy to see whether there is any relationship between the number of minutes it takes an office to see their customer on the first visit and the number of successful job placements the office gets every month. There may not be a relationship. Then again, perhaps a few of the customers "walk out" before being seen because of the long waits. It might be a good theory warranting further consideration.

One additional point. To keep our example simple, we have used limited data. We have listed only twelve sets of data from twelve offices. It is generally accepted that Scatter Diagrams should have a minimum of 40 sets of data to obtain valid results.

It is important that the data be selected simultaneously. This is rather obvious, but crucial enough to stress. To be valid, in our example our data should be taken from more than one month. If we were to obtain the same set of statistics for every month in the year, we would have 44 sets of data, exceeding the minimum generally accepted. We would, therefore, have more confidence in any relationship that appeared.

Step Four

Begin setting up the chart. Because there are two variables, you will need to decide where each set of data will be placed. Think about your data. In all likelihood it will appear that one variable is causing the other and would like to see if that is true. In the above example, we propose that if customers have to wait a long time to be seen on the first visit, they will walk out the door, and fewer placements will occur. It's worth investigating to see if a relationship exists. Additional study will be needed to see if there is a causal link.

Pick the variable suspected to be the cause to run along the horizontal axis, and the variable to be the effect to run along the vertical axis. Draw the chart accordingly. In our example, the horizontal axis will represent the average number of minutes taken to see a customer on the first visit, and the vertical axis will represent the average number of successful job placements per month.

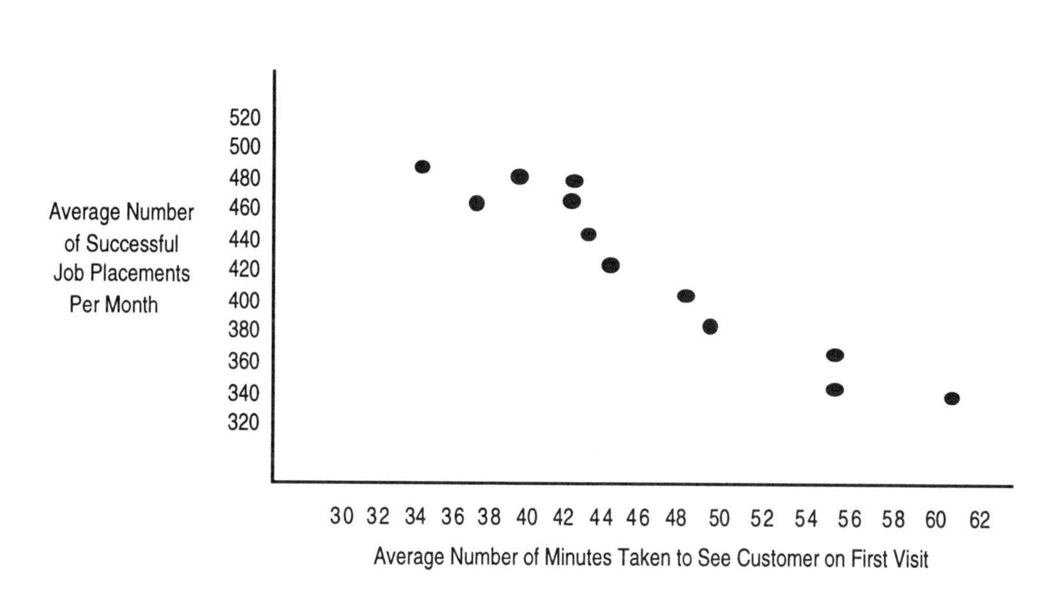

Step Five

Analyze the Scatter Diagram to see if a pattern is present and what that pattern means. There does seem to be a pattern in that the dots begin in the upper left hand corner and end in the lower right hand corner.

Compare the above diagram to the one below. The Scatter Diagram below shows absolutely no pattern or what statisticians call a "correlation." Correlation can be defined as, "a complementary, parallel or reciprocal relationship."

There is no apparent correlation associated with the next Scatter Diagram, while there appears to be one in the previous diagram.

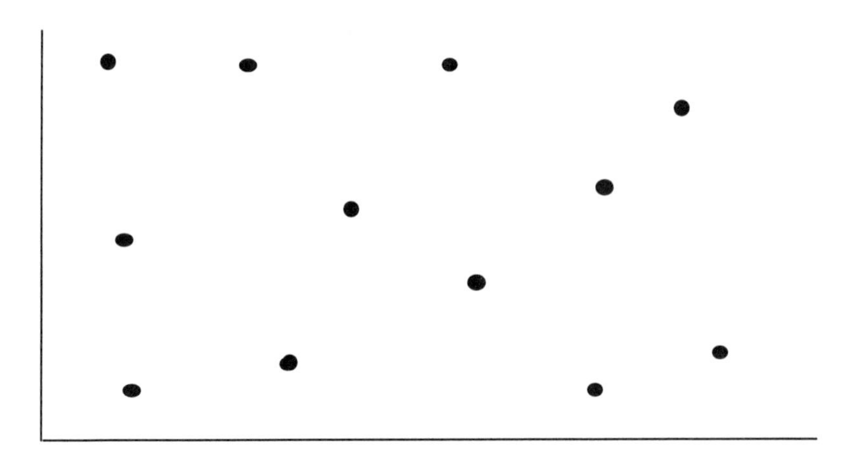

Note that the correlation in our example is a negative one. We say negative because the average number of minutes taken to see a customer on the first visit *increases* as the average number of successful placements *decreases*. This is in keeping with our theory that perhaps those offices that make customers wait longer have fewer customers to serve. However, correlation does not mean that one causes the other!

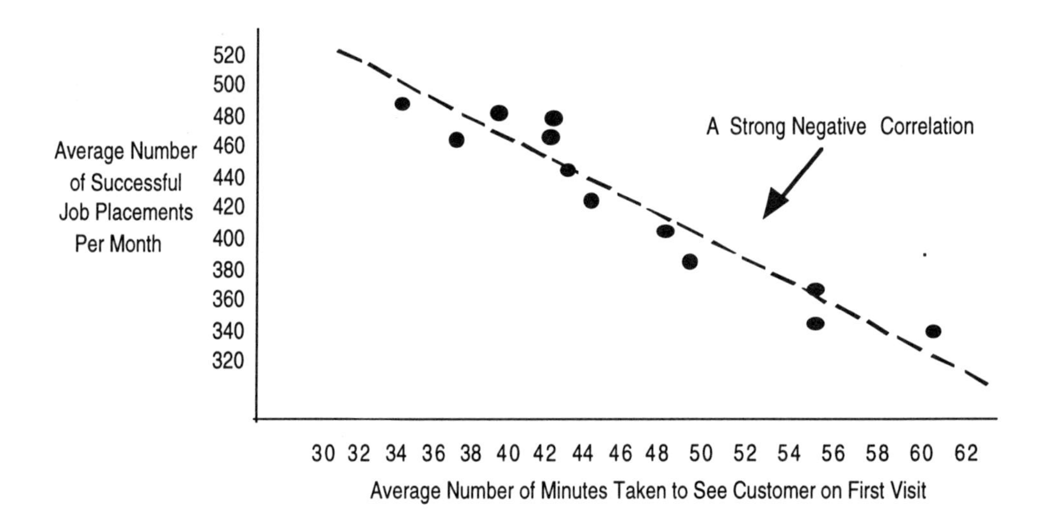

Note that when we place an imaginary dotted line through the points, we see that most come very close to the line. That is why it is called a "strong" negative correlation. The next Scatter Diagram would represent a "weak" negative correlation.

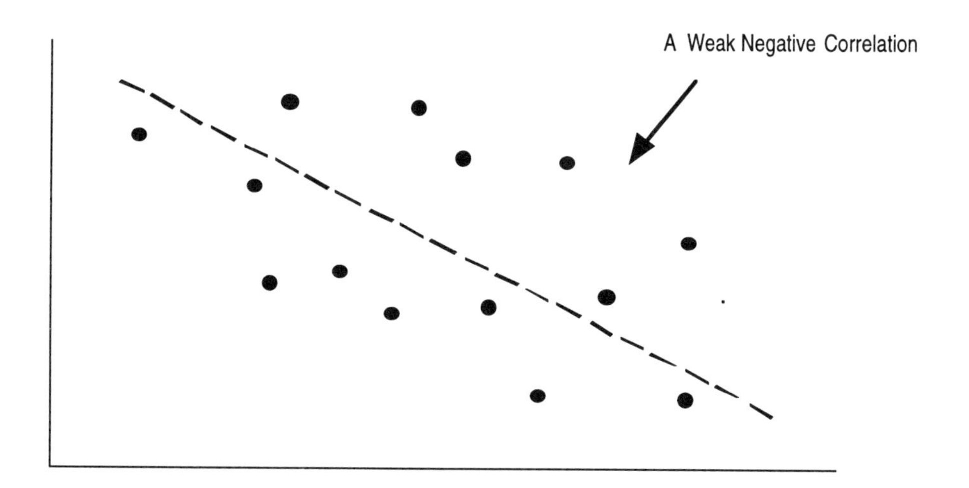

There is a pattern; it looks like a correlation, but it is a weak one at best. There may be a relationship, but there is no strong indication of one.

There is always the chance that the correlation could be a positive one. For example, suppose we found that as the average number of minutes taken to see a customer on the first visit increased, we also found an increase in the number of successful job placements! This might lead us to speculate that the customers who were really motivated "stuck it out" in the waiting room and eventually were placed in successful jobs. Perhaps in those offices where customers were seen quickly, there were more customers, but ones who merely wanted to talk about work and not really do it! The Scatter Diagram below represents a strong positive correlation.

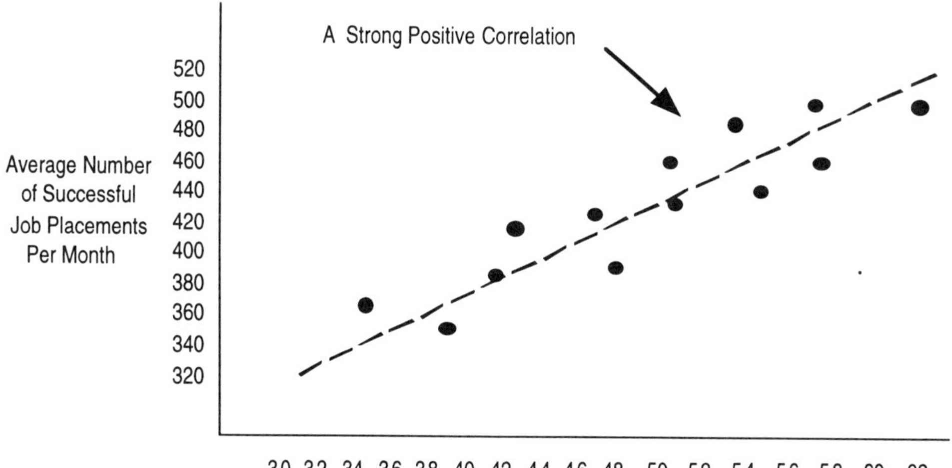

The Scatter Diagram below would represent a "weak" positive correlation.

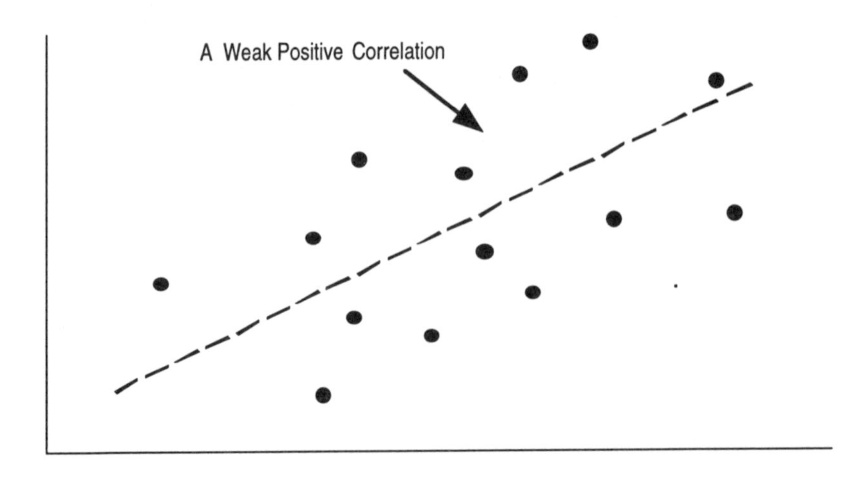

As with the previous weak negative correlation, there is a pattern; it looks like a correlation, but it is a weak one at best. There may be a relationship, but there is not strong indication of one.

Thus there are five common scatter diagrams you will probably encounter (strong negative, weak negative, strong positive, weak negative, and no correlation).

It is possible to find a scatter diagram that defies explanation, as in the one below. These complex scatter diagrams result on occasion for very valid reasons, but the explanation for them is beyond the scope of this book.

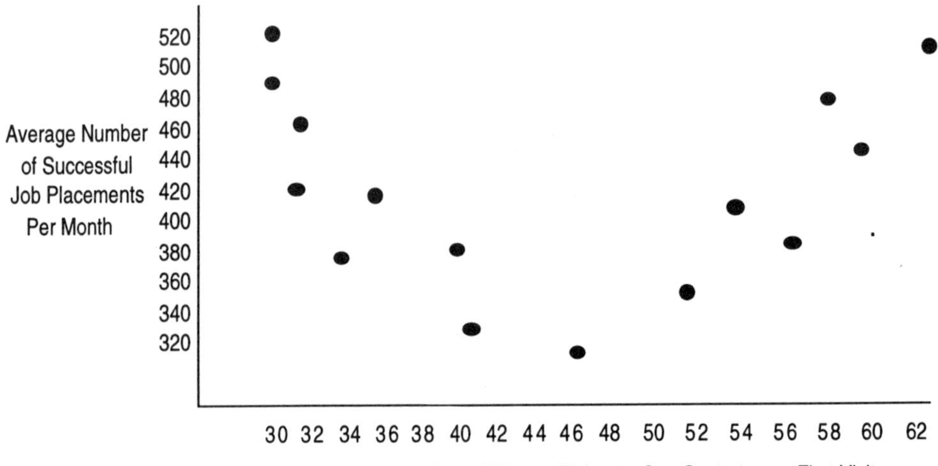

One last word is in order. Occasionally, you may get two or more entries with exactly the same values. This can be handled by circling the dot, or noting the multiple entries in a narrative right on the diagram.

Also make certain that you plot all the data and do not try to simplify the process by cutting out the extremes. To provide a valid interpretation all the data from the complete range must be shown. For example, we could see a strong negative relationship in the diagram above if we merely cut off any data that was above 46 minutes waiting time, or get a strong positive relationship if we cut off any data where customers waited less than 46 minutes.

It is exceptionally easy to misinterpret data.

21 SOLUTION STRATEGIES MATRIX

> ***"The real purpose of corrective action is to identify the best solution to a problem and eliminate the problem forever."***
>
> **—Philip B. Crosby**

Once the root cause(s) of a problem have been identified, the next responsibility of the team is to determine potential solutions. There are many effective approaches to problem resolution, but one that is exceptionally helpful is the **Solution Strategies Matrix.**

WHAT IS IT?

The Solution Strategies Matrix is a set of procedures that helps the team direct its efforts in a systematic way to consider the resources needed, cost to implement, payback period, management receptivity, difficulty to implement, etc. Using the system and matrix, the team is able to select the most appropriate solution.

WHY SHOULD IT BE USED?

It is not easy to select the best solution when confronted with several that appear to have merit. Decisions are always difficult, even when only one person is involved in the effort. When several team members consider solutions, each member comes with their own set of "baggage." Each has had different life experiences and, as a result, arguments can develop which do not lead to consensus or good decisions. The Solution Strategies Matrix is a tool that helps resolve this problem.

WHAT DOES A TEAM NEED TO USE IT?

The team should understand **brainstorming** and be willing to invest the time necessary to complete this important component of the process. A copy of a blank Solution Strategies Matrix should be available for each member. You will need several flip charts, markers and masking tape.

HOW DOE WE DO IT? WHAT ARE THE RULES?

Step One

Review each identified root cause (**cause and effect diagram**) to see if any can be combined. See if one possible solution will eliminate more than one cause. Determine if it will become necessary to consider more than one solution.

Step Two

Brainstorm possible solutions. Remember the rules of brainstorming:

- offer as many ideas as you can
- be creative
- build on others' ideas
- offer absolutely no criticism at any time
- place all ideas on a flip chart in the exact words of the contributor
- discuss the solutions after everyone is exhausted of ideas

Step Three

This step is optional. At this point, it is sometimes helpful for team members to interview others outside the team for possible ideas. This means that the team will have to stop its deliberations until everyone returns (perhaps a week later). Nevertheless, it is not a bad idea to have a break here anyway. Brainstorming sessions are often draining, and the team may appreciate an opportunity to interview others, to reflect upon what has been said thus far, and come back with renewed energy for step four.

Step Four

Complete the Solution Strategies Matrix. On the next page is a matrix that has been completed by a team considering four possible solutions to their problem. (A blank version follows for your personal use). Note that *each* member of the team individually completes the form *before* the team assigns values in a group discussion.

Also note that the last column identifies the "Desired Outcome." When a solution meets the criteria for this column, it earns a "+."

In this example:

- **Eliminates Root Cause**—there was agreement that every solution considered did eliminate the root cause which, obviously, is the desired outcome; all solutions earn a "+."
- **Percentage of Problem Solved**—solution #2 ranks highest; solution #4 lowest; only solution #2 earns a "+."
- **Can Team Implement**—all solutions can be implemented by the team; all solutions earn a "+."
- **Cost to Implement**—solution #2 is the least expensive—the desired outcome; give it a "+."

Solution Strategies Matrix

Solution Considerations	Possible Solutions				Desired Outcome
	1	*2*	*3*	*4*	
Eliminates Root Cause	*Yes*	*Yes*	*Yes*	*Yes*	Yes
Percentage of Problem Solved	*80%*	*95%*	*45%*	*75%*	Highest Percentage
Can Team Implement	*Yes*	*Yes*	*Yes*	*Yes*	Yes
Cost to Implement	*High*	*Low*	*High*	*Low*	Low $
Resources Needed	*More positions*	*None*	*More positions*	*Maybe More positions*	Identify
Resources Located	*Legislative*	*In-house*	*Legislative*	*In-house*	Identify
Payback Period	*Long-term*	*Immediate payback*	*Long-term*	*Immediate payback*	Time for Savings to Offset Cost
Creates New Problems	*?*	*No*	*Yes*	*Yes*	No
Number & Extent of New Problems	*Few*	*None*	*Major*	*Major*	Few/Minor
Are Affected Persons Committed	*Yes*	*Yes*	*No*	*No*	Yes
Management Receptivity	*Medium*	*High*	*Low*	*Low*	High
Difficulty to Implement	*Low*	*Low*	*High*	*High*	Low
Non-measureable Benefits	*None*	*Increased Morale*	*None*	*None*	Identify
Total	*6*	*13*	*3*	*4*	

- **Resources Needed**—solution #2 requires no additional resources; it earns a "+."
- **Resources Located**—two of the solutions require legislative action; solutions #2 & # 4 do not; solutions #2 & #4 earn a "+."
- **Payback Period**—two are long-term; two are immediate; give solutions #2 & #4 a "+."

- **Creates New Problems**—solution #2 is the clear winner; solutions #3 & #4 actually create new problems; we are uncertain about #1; solution #2 earns a "+."
- **Number & Extent of New Problems**—major problems develop with solutions #3 & #4; a few develop with #1; however, none develop with #2; solution #2 earns a "+."
- **Are Affected Persons Committed**—the answer is yes for solutions #1 and #2; no for #3 & #4; give #2 a "+."
- **Management Receptivity**—it is obvious that the team does not think that management will be too happy with solutions #3 & #4; furthermore solution #1 is just given a "medium" rank; once again solution #2 wins; give it a "+."
- **Difficulty to Implement**—Solutions #1 are apparently easy to implement, especially in comparison to solutions #3 and #4; give both #1 & #2 a "+."
- **Non-measurable benefits**—Only solution #2 comes in with a non-measurable benefit—"increased morale" and should therefore be given a "+."

When we add up the +'s, we find that solution #2 wins with a total of 13.

The Solution Strategies Matrix can be enhanced and refined as necessary by the team. After consideration, the team may decide that not all categories should be assigned the same weight. Perhaps some are far more important than others. For example, the team may reason that it is far more important that the suggestion actually eliminate the root cause of the problem than it is that the solution also has non-measurable benefits. Therefore, they may decide that this category (eliminate root cause) actually be weighted four times (because it is four times more important).

Weighing the categories in this manner, while helpful, adds a new dimension to the deliberations, however. Deciding weights can be difficult.

The categories are not written in stone, and teams may decide to eliminate some of those suggested, or add a few of their own. In many ways, the Solution Strategies Matrix resembles the **Priority Selection Worksheets** tool. Recall that one of the evaluation criteria listed then was that of "Importance to Customer." Perhaps consideration for the customer should also be a part of the Solution Strategies Matrix, with a category like "Customers Positively Impacted."

Step Five

Once the solution is selected, the team may wish to turn to the **Deming Cycle** to see what follows in the "Plan, Do, Check, Act" cycle. At this point an action plan with a **Milestone Chart** will assist the team in moving forward. This action plan will cover the pilot testing, evaluation and implementation strategies to determine how well the proposed solution works. The team then continues on around the cycle beginning with new identification of possible improvements.

Solution Strategies Matrix

Solution Considerations	Possible Solutions				Desired Outcome
	1	2	3	4	
Eliminates Root Cause					Yes
Percentage of Problem Solved					Highest Percentage
Can Team Implement					Yes
Cost to Implement					Low $
Resources Needed					Identify
Resources Located					Identify
Payback Period					Time for Savings to Offset Cost
Creates New Problems					No
Number & Extent of New Problems					Few/Minor
Are Affected Persons Committed					Yes
Management Receptivity					High
Difficulty to Implement					Low
Non-measureable Benefits					Identify
Total					

With the Solutions Strategies Matrix we conclude our Continual Improvement Tools and Methods section. The final two elements, Time Management and World Wide Web, are not actually tools, but you may find the information useful in TQM implementation.

A final thought on the tools presented. Please try them. Although they may appear difficult, they are not. The help they will give you as your team progresses will far exceed the effort you expend to use them. Every single text we have reviewed in the area of quality improvement stresses these tools. With them you identify and solve problems, improve processes, and can show how the improvements helped.

22 TIME MANAGEMENT

"We don't have the time..."
"We're too busy to meet..."
"There are too many customers coming in the front door..."

These are all statements made to avoid discussing continual improvement. They are difficult to argue with, for a visit to almost any office reveals that there are frequently too few resources and too few staff to handle the load.

How then, can we afford to take time to form teams and still fulfill our duties to the citizens we serve?

Consider the wood man who chops away with a dull ax, never taking time to sharpen it. He cuts fewer and fewer trees, but never stops chopping. The same is true in government. If we do not take time to improve the process, we are, like the wood man, not very effective as our ax dulls.

There are no easy answers, but we have a few suggestions. One of them is "time management." There are scores of books written on this subject. Government workers are not the only ones who are running short of time. Our new age seems to have failed in its promise of more leisure time with advances in technology. If anything, our lives have become far more complicated with the advent of cellular telephones, fax machines and beepers. Now we are working in our cars on the way to work, at work, on the way home, and at home because of these "advances." The scores of books on time management are filled with suggestions that can help a team.

WHAT IS IT?

Time management, or whatever the latest publications call it, is merely a series of steps we can take to manage the time we have to give us greater flexibility and control of activities in our lives.

WHY SHOULD IT BE USED?

We are all very busy in our work and at home. There are only 86,400 seconds in every day. There are methods that can help us organize and thus increase the discretionary time we can allocate to the things we really want to accomplish. In fact, many improvements in Total Quality Management relate to the better use of time and improved customer service centering on faster and more efficient provision of services.

WHAT DOES A TEAM NEED TO USE IT?

It needs only the desire to create more time for work productivity. There are many different techniques that have the same objective—to free up more time to accomplish what we consider important. There must be a desire to research these techniques through study. The discussion here will barely scratch the surface of what is available and will probably be outdated the moment it is printed. New ideas and concepts of time management are being developed daily. Yet most new ideas are actually revisions of old thinking.

HOW DO WE DO IT? WHAT ARE THE RULES?

There are no rules, or even **Steps**, that can be listed. There are principles that you can review. You can even use some of the tools we have already discussed to get a handle on management of your time.

Most approaches suggest that you first list your priorities. Some suggest that you rank your priorities as follows:

- A - must do
- B - beneficial, but not mandatory
- C - unnecessary—waste of time

Then, you should remove those activities that are a waste of time. What could these be?

Why not see if one of the tools we discussed earlier can help assess this. What if we took a team and asked them to **brainstorm** all the things that they did or processes they saw that fell into the unnecessary category? Perhaps, we could place these into a **cause and effect** diagram.

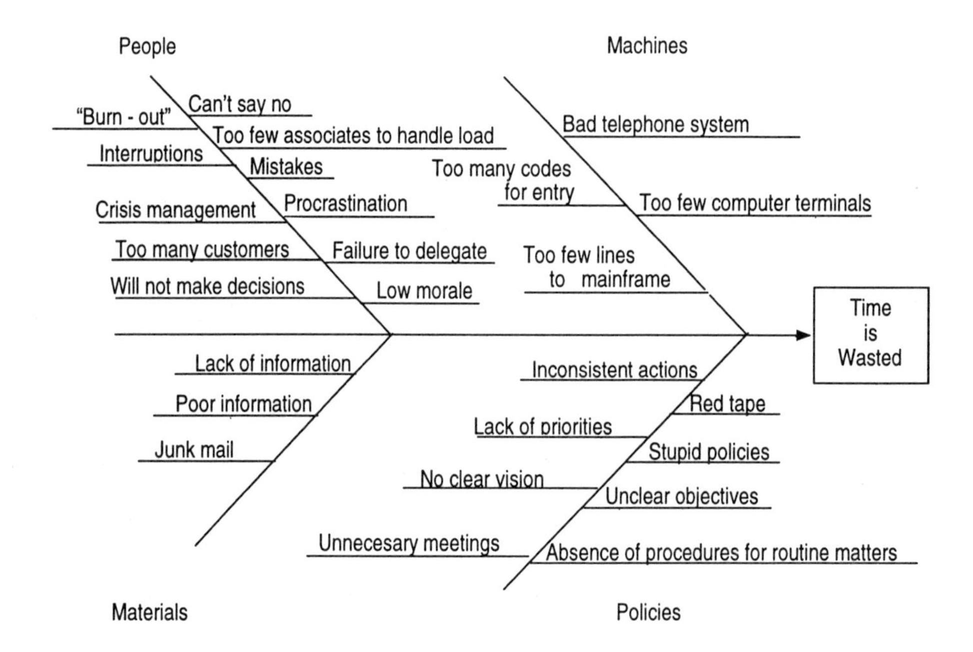

It is interesting how the use of the cause and effect diagram can help identify things that waste time in our lives. Also note that most time management strategies ask you to rank your priorities. We did this when we said to rank yours according to:

- A - must do
- B - beneficial, but not mandatory
- C - unnecessary - waste of time

This sounds a lot like what we did when we used the **priority selection worksheet** to decide what problems a team might like to address first. When we discussed that tool, we said that the most important step was that of selecting the right evaluation criteria to make certain that we selected a problem that could be addressed. Would it not be possible to develop evaluation criteria to see which "time wasters" we might be able to eliminate?

Perhaps, the first might be "Can we do it? Is it within our power to accomplish?" For example, the team identified the fact that there were "too many customers" coming in the door. It is hard to imagine this being identified as a time waster, but when people are frustrated, they may even attack the very reason for their agency's existence. What they probably meant is that there was no time left because they were overwhelmed with the number of customers coming in when so few staff were available to handle the load (which was another item identified under the "people" category). Nevertheless, we cannot in all honesty say that we have the power to stop the flow of customers and would not want to do this anyway.

In selecting the criteria to use to identify time wasters, we could include the following:

- Can we do it? Is it within our power to do so?
- Are there any federal or state laws that prevent us from doing it?
- Is it important to the customer?
- How much will it cost to eliminate it?
- Will elimination cause other problems?
- How difficult will it be to eliminate it?
- Will management support the elimination?
- What resources will be needed?

Taking each one of the identified causes of wasted time and answering the questions posed, our criteria will tell us which can be eliminated. Take, for example, "junk mail." Answer the questions:

1. Can we do it? Perhaps, but how?
2. Are there any federal or state laws that prevent us from doing it? Isn't all mail protected in some way? Check it out.
3. Is it important to the customer? Hardly.
4. How much will it cost to eliminate it? Depends upon what solution we come up with by the team.

5. Will elimination cause other problems? Only for the sender of the mail.
6. How difficult will it be to eliminate it? Again, it depends upon the solution we devise.
7. Will management support the elimination? Probably.
8. What resources will be needed? Again, it depends upon our solution. It appears that this might be a potential cause of wasted time to attack. The same will be true for many of the other identified causes. Other causes will be more difficult to eliminate.

Once we have identified those causes of wasted time that we can address, we return to our **Deming Cycle** to plan our strategies for change and develop our plan accordingly.

For example, suppose we decided that one time waster to be addressed by the team is the "unnecessary meetings." This item certainly meets the criteria. Our plan might include a brainstorming session to determine what makes the meetings unnecessary. Who is calling these meetings and why? How many unnecessary meetings have there been? What is the criteria for labeling the meetings unnecessary? What would make the meetings meaningful?

Potential solutions may be discussed by the team. Effective and meaningful meetings do not just happen. There are ways to make meetings valuable and not a waste of time. Perhaps some training in what makes a good meeting (having a purpose, an agenda, etc.) is in order.

These solutions are then piloted in accordance with the Deming Cycle. This systematic approach to the elimination of time wasters will work.

Many of the other causes of wasted time need not take the deliberations of a team. A few may respond to training, i.e., training managers how to delegate, how to make decisions, etc. There are some things in our work life that we already know how to cure. What it takes is not a process improvement team, but an administration with the desire to have a world-class agency and the strength and courage to take necessary action.

You can take control of your time. As a matter of fact, you are the only one who can. Start today.

23 WORLD WIDE WEB

We add the World Wide Web here because we firmly believe that it will prove exceptionally useful to teams addressing process improvement. It represents the future, for through this resource, you and your team will be able to access the very latest information not only on continual improvement, but perhaps on the very process you are improving.

WHAT IS IT?

The World Wide Web is a user-friendly interface into the Internet. The World Wide Web, also known as WWW, is part of the Internet that links all servers who offer access to hypermedia-based information and documentation. The WWW makes it easier for us to get information from thousands, even millions, of computers throughout the world. All of these computers are linked together so that anyone with a desktop computer, whether it be an IBM running MS-DOS, a Macintosh or even computers that run other systems, can gather data. You merely select with your mouse an item, picture, or sentence on the screen, and you immediately call and get that information or download information to a personal computer.

WHY SHOULD IT BE USED?

It is an excellent way to keep up with what is happening. It provides focused information search. The information is current, immediately accessible and interactive. You can obtain much more information that you will ever be able to use.

WHAT DOES A TEAM NEED TO USE IT?

All you need is a computer, appropriate software and a way to access the service. All of this information is available at your library, local software store or from a management information specialist. You may already have it installed in your agency. Just about every federal, state, and local government agency has a great deal of their information and documents available on the WWW.

HOW DO WE DO IT? WHAT ARE THE RULES?

The best way to describe the process is to show you (see page 137) what we retrieved when we were "surfing the WWW" just having fun. We were at the White House home page (the home page is the first page at a site and generally has a number of items underlined to take us to other pages). At the White House, we clicked on "Executive Reports." That took us to a page with several reports, one of which was "National

Performance Review." We clicked on that and found the page that appears on the next page. Note that several lines of type are underlined. When we point our mouse to one of these and click on it, we get it! Some even contain an audio track. By clicking on the words "Statement by the President," we obtained an audio message through our computer's speaker from the President.

From Red Tape to Results

Creating a Government That Works Better & Costs Less

Report of the National Performance Review

Vice President Al Gore, September 7, 1993

Statement by the President (audio)

Statement by the Vice-President (audio)

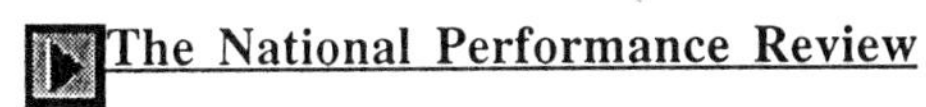
The National Performance Review

- **Supporting Materials to the Review**

- Community IdeaNet
- Remarks by the President and Vice-President in presenting the National Performance review
- Initial Announcement of the organization of the NPR
- Background Briefing by Senior Administration Officials
- Remarks by the President and Vice-President at the GSA Warehouse
- Press Briefing on Reinventing Government with David Osborne and John Sharp
- Ash Receivers, Tobacco (Desk type)
- Letter to the president

- Monographs relating to Actions resulting from NPR

About the hypertext version

Back to the Government home page

SUGGESTED READINGS

Aguayo, Rafael. *Dr. Deming: The American Who Taught the Japanese About Quality.* Secaucus, NJ: Carol Publishing Group, 1990.

Aubrey, C.A. and P.K. Felkins. *Teamwork: Involving People in Quality and Productivity Improvement*. White Plains, NY: Quality Resources, 1988.

Beckhard, R. and W. Pritchard. *Changing the Essence, The Art of Creating and Leading Fundamental Change in Organizations.* San Francisco, CA: Jossey-Bass Publishers, 1992.

Belbin, R.M. *Management Teams: Why They Succeed or Fail.* New York: Wiley, 1981.

Brassard, Michael., ed. *The Memory Jogger.* Methuen, Mass: GOAL/QPC, 1988.

Buchholz, S. and T. Roth. *Creating the High-Performance Team.* New York: Wiley, 1987.

Byham, William C. *Zapp!: The Lightning of Empowerment: How to Improve Productivity, Quality and Employee Satisfaction.* New York, NY: Harmony Books, 1990.

Carr, David K. *Excellence in Government: Total Quality Management in the 1990's.* Arlington, VA: Coopers & Lybrand, 1990.

Crosby, Philip B. *Completeness: Quality for the 21st Century.* New York, NY: Dutton, 1992.

———. *Quality is Free: The Art of Making Quality Certain.* New York, NY: McGraw-Hill, 1979.

———. *Quality Without Tears: The Art of Hassel-Free Management.* New York, NY: McGraw-Hill, 1984.

———. *Running Things: The Art of Making Things Happen.* New York, NY: McGraw-Hill, 1986.

———. *The Eternally Successful Organization.* New York, NY: Penguin Books, 1988.

Cullen, Joe and Jack Hollingum. *Implementing Total Quality*. Bedford, MA: IFS Publications, 1987.

Deming, W. Edwards. *Out of the Crisis*. Cambridge, MA: MIT, Center for Advanced Engineering Study, 1988.

———. *The New Economics*. Cambridge, MA: MIT, Center for Advanced Engineering Study, 1993.

Feigenbaum, A.V. *Total Quality Control*. New York, NY: McGraw-Hill, 1991.

Francis, Dave. *Improving Work Groups: A Practical Manual for Team Building*. La Jolla, CA: University Associates, 1979.

Gabor, Andrea. *The Man Who Discovered Quality: How W. Edwards Deming Brought the Quality Revolution to America*. New York, NY: Times Books, 1991.

Gitlow, Howard S. *The Deming Guide to Quality and Competitive Position*. Englewood Cliffs, NJ: Prentice-Hall, 1987.

Harrington, H. James. *The Improvement Process: How America's Leading Companies Improve Quality*. New York, NY: McGraw-Hill, 1987.

Harrington-Mackin, Deborah. *The Team Building Tool Kit*. New York, NY: American Management Association, 1994.

Hess, K., ed. *Creating the High Performance Team*. New York: Wiley, 1987.

Hunt, V. Daniel. *Quality in America: How to Implement a Competitive Quality Program*. Homewood, IL: Business One Irwin, 1992.

Hutchins, David C. *Achieve Total Quality*. Englewood Cliffs, NJ: Director Books, 1991.

Imai, Masaki. *Kaizen: The Key to Japan's Competitive Success*. New York, NY: Free Press, 1986.

Ishikawa, Kaoru. *Guide to Quality Control*. White Plains, NY: Quality Resources, 1986.

Jablonski, Joseph R. *Implementing Total Quality Management: An Overview*. San Diego, CA: Pfeiffer, 1991.

Juran, J. M. *Juran on Leadership for Quality: An Executive Handbook*. New York, NY: Free Press, 1989.

———. *Juran on Planning for Quality: An Executive Handbook*. New York, NY: Free Press, 1988.

Juran, Joseph M. with Frank M. Gryna. *Juran's Quality Control Handbook*, 4th Edition. New York, NY: McGraw-Hill, 1988.

Lam, K.D. *Total Quality Management: A Resource Guide.* Colorado Springs, CO: Air Academy Press, 1990.

Lewis, Ralph G. and Douglas H. Smith. *Total Quality Management in Higher Education.* Delray Beach, FL: St. Lucie Press, 1994.

Naisbett, John. *Megatrends 2000: Ten New Directions for the 1990's.* New York, NY: Morrow, 1990.

Oakland, John S. *Total Quality Management.* New York, NY: Nichols Publishing, 1989.

Osborne, David. *Re-Inventing Government: How the Entrepreneurial Spirit is Transforming the Public Sector.* Reading, MA: Addison-Wesley, 1992.

Ryan, Kathleen D. and Daniel K. Oestreich. *Driving Fear Out of the Workplace.* San Francisco, CA: Jossey-Bass, 1991.

Saylor, James H. *TQM Field Manual.* New York, NY: McGraw-Hill, 1991.

Scherkenbach, William W. *The Deming Route to Quality and Productivity: Road Maps and Roadblocks.* Milwaukee, WI: ASQC Quality Press, 1991.

Scholtes, Peter R. *The Team Handbook: How to Use Teams to Improve Quality.* Madison, WI: Joiner, 1988.

Senge, Peter M. *Managing Quality: A Primer for Middle Managers.* Reading, MA: Addison-Wesley Publishers, 1992.

Shores, A. Richard. *Survival of the Fittest: Total Quality Control and Management Evolution.* Milwaukee, WI: ASQC Quality Press, 1988.

Stratton, A. Donald. *An Approach to Quality Improvement that Works.* Milwaukee, WI: ASQC Quality Press, 1991.

Tague, Nancy R. *The Quality Toolbox.* Milwaukee, WI: ASQC Quality Press, 1995.

Townsend, Patrick L. *Commit to Quality.* New York, NY: Wiley, 1990.

Varney, Glenn H. *Building Productive Teams: An Action Guide and Resource Book.* San Francisco, CA: Jossey-Bass, 1989.

Walton, Mary. *The Deming Management Method.* New York, NY: Perigee Books, The Putnam Publishing Group, 1986.

Wellins, Richard S., William C. Byham, and Jeanne M. Wilson. *Empowered Teams: Creating Self-Directed Work Groups that Improve Quality, Productivity and Participation.* San Francisco, CA: Jossey-Bass Publishers, 1991.

Westland, Cynthia Lane. *Quality: The Myth and the Magic.* Milwaukee, WI: ASQC Quality Press, 1990.

Woodcock, M. and D. Francis. *Organizational Development Through Team-building.* Aldershot, England: Gower, 1981.

INDEX

E

F

G

H

I

J

K

L

M

N

O

Q

R

S

X